Once Upon a Time

Once Upon a Time

A PERSONAL GUIDE TO TELLING
AND WRITING YOUR OWN STORY

for Adrienn

Ross Talarico

Ross Talari

9/05

STORY LINE PRESS Ashland, Oregon

Published by Story Line Press,
Three Oaks Farm, PO Box 1240
Ashland, OR 97520-0055

www.storylinepress.com

This publication was made possible thanks in part to the generous support of
our individual contributors.

Cover art: Edward Potthast, *Afternoon Fun*, Oil on canvas, 24 x 30 inches,
Collection of The Butler Institute of American Art, Youngstown, Ohio

Text design by Lisa Garbutt, www.RaraAvisGraphicDesign.com

Library of Congress Cataloging-in-Publication Data

Talarico, Ross, 1945-
  Once upon a time : a personal guide to telling and writing your own story
/ By Ross Talarico.
     p. cm.
  ISBN 1-58654-042-4 (alk. paper)
  1. Oral biography. 2. Autobiography—Authorship. I. Title.
CT22.T35 2004
808'.06692—dc22
                              2004013009

For my mom, Regina
Her one story: being there ॐ

Contents

Preface

THERE ARE SOME BOOKS THAT PROVIDE EVEN THE AUTHOR WITH A sudden awareness of where one's life has led. This, to me, is one of those books. My attachment to people, to communities, has always equaled or surpassed my love for literature. I have to say, candidly, that has not been an endearing quality in the world of American letters I encountered as a young poet. When I spoke out against elitism, I was labeled a rebel—and I came to understand that my interest in literature along with the role of writers as active change agents in our culture was not shared by many of my counterparts. Interestingly, I became America's only full-time "Writer-in-Residence" under the auspices of a city-government, and I was happy to see that the book that describes the effect of that position on an entire community, *Spreading The Word: Poetry and the Survival of Community in America*, was given an extraordinary award and honored by others, mainly educators who were looking for ways to make literature relevant and meaningful, not by writers who felt comfortable with their isolated status.

Subsequently, my audience became "educators" and "scholars," not really reflecting my own view of myself. The truth is, I am a poet, and it is my sense of the poetic core of the stories of ordinary people and their desires to express themselves passionately that makes me who I am. And that is what this book is about. Yes, this appeal to others to take the time and make a guided effort to not only express themselves, but to share their stories for the sake of breaking down barriers of prejudice, bias, and intolerance, this appeal reflects the direction my life has been going for many years now. My hope is that this book will lead to the network of storytelling groups I describe within these pages, a harmony among readers, something I have always envisioned, and now think is entirely possible.

Ross Talarico, September, 2004

Acknowledgments

Grateful acknowledgment is given to the following publications where some of the essays, articles, and narratives originally appeared:

Poetics/Politics: Radical Aesthetics for the Classroom, ed. by Amitava Kumar, St. Martins Press, 1999: "America's New Storytellers: The Corporate Classroom and Its Lessons on Life."

The North American Review, Vol. 286, No. 6, Dec. 2001: "Native American, Truly American."

Ambassador Magazine, Spring, 2000: "The New Shoes."

Calling Home: Working Class Women's Writings, ed. by Janet Zandy, Rutgers University Press, 1990: "Train Ride," "My Certificate in Negro History," "Hands: A Love Poem."

Upstate Magazine, Gannett Newspapers, July, 1988: "Spring Vows," "The Photograph," "The Mansion," "Convertible 1928," "Youth."

Democrat & Chronicle, Gannett Newspapers: "Silver Dollars, Silver Memories"; "What To Look For in a Tree"; "The Game"; "Chris Tuck's Quiet Vision"; "Lyell Avenue"; "The Coolin' Board (The Day Our Daddy Came Home)."

Once Upon a Time

ONE

Telling a Story:
The Incidental
Self-Revelation

LET ME SHARE A STORY WITH YOU. NOT A VERY SIGNIFICANT
one by any means. Just something that's stayed with me over
the years.

What to Look For in a Tree
Two weeks or so before Christmas every year, there in
Rochester, New York, in a poor but adventurous Italian-
American neighborhood as the December snow sparkled
through the early evening air, I remember donning my wool
scarf and picking up my gloves off the heater vent on the dining room floor, and following my dad down the street and
around the corner to Bay Street. Mr. Gunther's wrap-around
porch was strung with lights, as was his driveway and his yard,
where the Christmas trees, half frozen, flecked with snow, lay
against the house and garage, the others just lying on the
ground. From about five years earlier, when I was seven or
eight, I had been going with my father to choose a tree. And I
remember the ritual well.

My father was not much of an outdoorsman. He worked in a
shoe factory, something, I would come to understand, that gave
him no pleasure in life, and he read books, especially Ellery
Queen mysteries. We were the only family in the neighborhood,

come to think of it, to have bookshelves built into the walls, and except for a couple of St. Jude statues my mother beckoned in times of need, they were filled with books. My two older sisters read every night in fact, and almost reluctantly, I picked up the habit. No, my father preferred the kitchen table at night, the instant coffee, and the Chesterfield cigarette always there between his fingers, the smoke steady like that from a small campfire. Outside, even in the midst of winter, even with the big flakes of Canadian snow falling over our neighborhood, he would never wear a hat, and one of my aunts always said that's what made his hair turn so white so early in his life. But I didn't think so. I think he was worried about things, though he'd never say so. He always seemed so calm and cheerful, even when they made him stay in bed to cure his ulcers.

Yes, I remember the ritual: my father, the snow in his hair and melting on his wire-rimmed glasses, holding each tree up straight to check the height (it had to be about six feet), leaving room for the stand underneath and the paper angel my sister made on top; tipping it against the ground a couple of times to shake the snow off and let the branches settle, and pushing back the balsam needles to make sure it hadn't been cut too soon. And then, if the trunk was straight and not too thin, my dad would bring it over to Mr. Gunther and pay him two dollars. He'd never ask how much the tree cost; he just gave him two bucks. That was good enough for Mr. Gunther.

When I was sixteen, my father was sick in bed in December, and my mother sent me alone one night to pick out the Christmas tree up on Bay Street. I remember standing under a silvery snow, eyeing up all those trees lying against the side of Mr. Gunther's house, and feeling for the first time in my life a responsibility, a worry, an obligation I didn't expect to experience for some time to come.

I held up one tree, then another. I shook the branches, making sure, as my father had taught me, that there was enough space to allow ornaments and icicles to hang properly. I checked the straightness of the trunk, and, like my father, I bushed back the balsam needles with my thumb to see if they remained firm. When I picked out the right tree, I brought it up to Mr. Gunther. "How much?" I asked.

"Two fifty," he replied. I pulled out all the money my mother had given me—two dollar bills. Mr. Gunther smiled and took them out of my hand. "That's a fine tree you picked out," he said pushing the tree toward me. "You tell your dad to get well real quick." But my father never did get well. And the next year I went alone again for the family tree, and the following year, the year my dad died, I was even more alone measuring the trunk and the space between the branches.

Now, how many years later, I take my own two sons. I try to tell them what to look for in a tree, but I still don't think I can tell them why. Perhaps it's simple; a Christmas tree is not special in itself. What gives it meaning is the care with which we adorn it. The lights, the ornaments, the star on the top, the communal effort, are celebrations of our spirit, which, to be honest, often escapes me during the year. For me, the holiday takes its meaning from the memory of a time when it wasn't what was under the tree that enriched us (I have a tough time, in fact, remembering what gifts I received), but the tree itself, a tree which lit up the living room, a tree which glowed in our hearts because it represented a family's best efforts in celebrating our small space in the world.

Perhaps I can't articulate any more than anyone else my ambiguous feelings about the Christmas season. But I can assure you that I can pick out a tree. And I can tell you if there is a spirit that comes with the holiday, it's always right beside me, like a shadow, as I see myself dragging the tree home down Bay Street and around the corner to my house. And by now you know a little something about me, so if I happen to say Merry Christmas, you'll know the words come from conviction, and not from routine. ࠺

WHAT GOES INTO A STORY? AND WHY MIGHT ONE TELL AS STORY in the first place?

A story is an attempt to isolate a moment. It tries to capture that moment, and, by recreating it, allows others to realize both its universal application to human experience and its meaning. However, it's not as simple as it sounds. Since it is not enough to merely restate facts alone, the storyteller becomes, in effect, an expert at invention-even if that story-teller is being as truthful as he or she can be. The measure of success for a good story is how true it is to our emotions, how accurately it reflects the life we all live. After all, without human understanding, experience, in the words of author Eudora Welty, is "the worst kind of emptiness."

This book will present several stories by ordinary people, including several by me in an attempt to follow the intriguing ways in which stories beget other stories in an attempt to dis-cover more and more meaning out of reflection and articulation. It is not just "natural" to want to tell our stories to each other, it is a kind of compulsion if we want to understand how we live and why we behave the way we do; more so, storytelling has been, throughout the history of mankind, the way we pass on wisdom from one generation to another. It is a means to survival if we mean by "survival" an enriched life which optimizes human potential for understanding, civility, and love. It is no small matter. And the crucial point upon which this book will focus is: we can't leave our storytelling in the hands of others anymore. The next chapter in this book, America's New Storytellers: The Corporate Classroom and Its Lessons on Life, begins to describe the dangers when we count on others, ignore our storytelling instincts and skills, and, most importantly, when we can no longer tell the difference between a "story" and a "non-story."

But this book will attempt to do more than present stories and alert the reader to the dangers of losing our abilities to tell, listen to, and discover the meaning of our own stories. It will be a guide, a "how to" manual, so the reader can engage in a communal effort with family and friends to tell, develop, and record stories that give us not only pleasure, which is an essential element of all this activity, but a sense of values as we take the time to reflect upon and assert deep-felt personal convictions that do not always emerge in a fast-paced culture that counts on slogans, clichés, and a bombardment of media images to convey fleeting impressions that often substitute for traditional wisdom. Every time an elderly person dies, as I've said before, it's like a library burning down.

IF YOU LOOK AGAIN AT THE INCIDENTAL STORY WITH WHICH I begin this book, you will begin to see some essential elements of storytelling. Obviously, it is a story about my father and some aspect of my boyhood. Although it's ostensibly about choosing a Christmas tree, that is the vehicle through which the more essential story emerges—the story about caring and love within a family. There is a very important concept that every storyteller knows, either consciously or subconsciously: the more essential qualities that give stories true meaning, the considerations and observations of abstractions that are almost impossible to understand by mere statement, such as *love, grief, hope* etc., those qualities are communicated indirectly through the vehicle, or subject matter of the story—the who, when, where, and how's which are fundamental to any good tale. So that's the storyteller's immediate concern: to concentrate on details, to try to bring the listener or the reader into the story's setting-to engage the audience as immediately as possible.

Now the last thing I want to do is make this book sound like a textbook. After being a professor for the last twenty years, that's the last thing I want to do! I've had enough of the separation we somehow have artificially imposed upon our culture between "literature" and a good story. But a few things should be understood from the beginning, and one essential concept is that we pay attention to the details of our subject matter, and for all good purposes, those details are equated with the story itself.

So of course I begin very traditionally, and by the end of the introduction, or the first paragraph, you know where and when the story is unfolding, and what we're about to do as I "follow" my dad to Mr. Gunther's house to pick out a tree. The wonderful thing about remembering detail is that every story gets sidetracked by them, and many times in wonderful and meaningful ways (that's how the subconscious emerges). In the second paragraph, I feel compelled to begin describing my father and my family to some small degree, and of course it's in those details that the story begins to make itself more clear both to me, the teller and to you, the listener/reader. The few details that emerge begin to reveal something unique about our family, the only family on the block, apparently, to have books and read regularly—a family involved in the world of reflection, imagination, and, perhaps, conceptual-thinking—elements, ironically, of storytelling itself. We see too that there are details that seem to have an insistence of their own in this case, the fact that my father suffered from ulcers and hated his job in the shoe factory. They serve, although again this is the subconscious emerging, to give the story some depth, some honesty, providing a fact important to the storyteller to give his story tone (the attitude the storyteller takes toward his/her subject matter). It becomes, although the storyteller might not know it as he is relating his tale, a *foreshadowing* to the father's sickness later on. It also provides us with a sense of *ambiguity*, something effective storytellers make good use of, a way of admitting other possible interpretations to parts of the story, happiness tempered by grief, hope tempered by disbelief—feeling two emotions at one time. It makes the story more viable, more real.

Of course I have to conclude the story line about my dad buying the tree so I can get to the second part of this story, going to Mr. Gunther's by myself when my dad gets sick and is bed-ridden. Getting a brief but vivid look at both my father and the tree he picks out is important to the story. Details! The young boy's parallel experience of buying a tree is important because this eventually will be a story about passing on not just a technique for choosing a tree, but a perspective on what constitutes a warm family feeling during a holiday that is often overwhelmed by a consumer attitude toward the Christmas season. Fittingly, this "ritual" is passed along to my children, and before we realize it, the story of choosing a Christmas tree transcends itself until within that story we recognize values that probably inspired the storyteller in the first place, however subconscious those thoughts might have been.

The purpose of this introduction, subsequently, is to state simply, at the beginning of this testament to storytelling, that by analysis we might become more aware of what goes into a story and why. We'll get more instructive as we go on—you will learn how to tell your stories and expound on their meanings after the fact. But before we go on to other stories and aspects of storytelling, let's go onto to a provocative look at how our culture makes it difficult to consider even the simplest, most fundamental notions of this book.

TWO

America's New Storytellers: The Corporate Classroom and its Lessons on Life

PEOPLE'S INDIVIDUAL STORIES ARE THE BEST-KEPT SECRETS IN the country! Not only are they not expressed and shared as they have been in every culture leading up to ours, our people have lost the ability to tell their own stories, have lost writing, story-telling and critical skills, have lost interest in articulation of personal experiences, and everyday count more and more on generic story-substitutes and media hype in order to create a sense of identity. There is something very suspicious about a system that not only tolerate writers, but subsidizes them through universities and elsewhere, the same system that has not only obliterated the true storytelling sensibility in this country, but which has incorporated the elements of storytelling and subverted them through corporate means. What I'm saying is that every year in America writers multiply themselves, especially through university "writing" programs and the like with a diminishing correlative effect on community and society itself.

The "art" gets more imitative, less distinct, more elitist, less socially, politically, and culturally aware. The writer gets more self-centered (and isolated and eventually alienated), more interested in the existential act of performance, the effect of expression immediate rather than reflective, the focus personality rather then the universal awareness that goes beyond personality. There has been, in effect, despite all the attempts at summer writing conferences, despite all the literary magazines that continually sprout, a subversion of traditional literary and storytelling efforts, like everything else in the culture of appearances and surfaces by a system that provides, as critic Eliot Weinberger puts it, "a sealed cage with plenty of cheese."

What's missing is the connection to ordinary people and day-to-day experiences through which we come to identify both ourselves and our world. *Media display* is the substitute. *Consumerism* fills the void. I've always believed that at the core of literature, of any art, was the notion of a celebration based on thorough, honest examinations of human existence and predicament, even if a resolution echoes the words of the German poet Goethe, who says, "if I have to live a life of anguish and fear, I thank God at least I have a voice to speak of it." To know that voice, to use it and share it with others is the essence of poetry, form the Greeks to Shakespeare, from Whitman to... to... That's just it—something doesn't change, we need a voice, one that speaks at once to both heart and mind, something at once both immediate and universal. And that voice, indeed, continues to exist, brilliantly, in fact, on the surface of our needs—the strong image, the musical phrase, the visual jolt and the sound bite. It is the voice of the corporate, commercial enterprise, employing all the storytelling component except for reflection, insight, analysis, etc., since those things are not part of the corporate operati. In other words, as we are bound endlessly by the provocative images and lyrical phrases of television commercials and magazine ads, edified by their apparent relevance, the recognition (if nothing more) of legitimate social themes as they tickle our subconscious, we go through the motions of literacy appraisal, the brief economic display of sound and sight, a hint of conflict, and the illusion of epiphany; but... on closer examination, we have been manipulated by an experience that helps us deny our humanistic possibilities—slick, striking, sensational campaigns that exploit our fears, anger, hostilities and anxieties: in other words, a notion completely antithetical to the literary equivalent, the affirmation of life that leads to empathy, insight, and an understanding that might put the true value of consumerism into proper perspective.

To make a closer examination of "perspectives," I'll take a critical look at some of America's most popular story substitutes, a closer reading and analysis of three popular, successful commercials created by the unlimited budgets of corporate enterprises—namely McDonalds, General Motors, and Coca Cola. These represent the work of the "new storytellers" in America. They also represent, there's no denying it, the brilliant effectiveness of big-business, of advertising in general, where no one spends one or two million dollars in production costs and air time without a guarantee, based on numerous indicators, that the effort will more than pay for itself in consumer response. Then I'll look at three stories that correlate subject-wise and to some degree thematically with the three commercials. These mini-stories were told or written by ordinary people, not professionals—a white male in his seventies, a white woman in her eighties, and a black teenager. The three writings were produced in community center workshops on a volunteer basis.

There was, a year or two back, a series of McDonalds commercials which served to induce in our conscious and subconscious minds the memorable, catchy, lyrical phrase, *you deserve a break today.* They generally employed, not surprisingly, family scenes, images and settings which brought us immediately to a consideration of one of the most pressing of our social dilemmas—recognition of traditional family values in a culture of dysfunctional families. The particular commercial I'll allude to begins with a scene inside a house where a father is working on a door frame and a son about five years old approaches him as he's kneeling and obviously consumed by some repair. We are, as viewers, almost immediately edified in the sense that we are exposed to a man, a father, "taking care" of his house. It is, of course, a symbol as well as an image, the gesture representing the head of the household attending the entranceway to the home itself. In a few seconds we will see, if we critically review the commercial, a wonderful irony emerge, one worthy of our sense of literary merit, since it is not, after all, an entrance we are to be concerned with, but an exit from the home. The young boy comes up to the father and suggest some idle social activity—first playing ball, then some other activity as he approaches his dad again; but each time the father rejects the suggestion by saying *no*, and *not now, I'm busy*. We can all relate to that scene, and if we had to, can add a hundred other items which, in a world of being too busy with work, thus too busy with the growing agenda of general repairs, commitments, and exhaustive responsibilities, kept us from spending the appropriate time with our children in a nourishing home environment. Again, this is edification—we recognize a theme and the commercial certainly seems to consider it. Finally—don't forget, we are seeing the entire commercial unfolding in thirty seconds or so—the boy comes up and asks *Can we go to McDonalds?* Suddenly, the music swells, the expression of both the child and the father change, and, magically, we are suddenly removed from the setting of hostility and non-communication; in other words, as we begin to hear (and sing along in our mind) the lyrical music of the orchestrated phrase, *you deserve a break today*, we leave the house. The scene that emerges as the music begins to dominate is, of course, a McDonalds restaurant, where the father and son are now cheery and talkative, sitting there, as one might in another culture in an earlier existence at a kitchen table at home, enjoying each other's company. The camera zooms back, capsulating the full environment, more families eating, laughing, ordering hamburgers and fries, all under the friendly golden arches canopy of McDonalds. The viewer is inundated with the warmth of knowing that family values still exist, despite the frightening impact of homes without dialogue, without face to face family dinners, without one parent or the other, or without parents at all. We have been edified by the extraordinary power of the "poetic" elements of the commercial, the stark swift images, the economy of words sustained by music, the quick juxtaposition of conflicting emotions—the muted sadness and the concluding spectacle of animated joy, the epiphany, and the celebratory moment of the communion of souls. It leaves us feeling terribly satisfied, and why wouldn't it, since we are spared, almost entirely, of any personal concern whatsoever as far as the issue that certainly is the basis of the commercial in the first place, a concern that, in the hands of the "storytellers" of these corporate advertisers, has been totally overwhelmed, concealed, and dissipated by the end of the commercial.

But if we were to "read" the commercial, as we might a poem or a short story, we might utilize our powers of analysis, and come up with the real message of the commercial, which is responsive to the fears and anxieties which engage us in the first place: if it is too stressful to deal with the serious issues of dysfunctional family life in America, come to McDonalds—for only at McDonalds can you experience old time family values as you know them, smiling dads and moms cheerfully providing you with the sustenance of Big Macs. The irony I alluded to earlier is evident in a critical reading of the commercial, the doorway leads *out of the house, not in*, for only in the corporate world of McDonalds can family values have the opportunity to materialize. The message is sinister, a stark contrast to thee mood of the viewer who is already singing along with the well-known lyric that signifies the corporate entity. Such a sate of mind needs nothing more than a continual menu of neural stimuli and an assurance that everything is fine in designated shelters. In contrast, let me share with you a memoir also written on the subject of father and son, one written by a man in his seventies remembering his father. His name is Joe Pohl, and this was written in a storytelling workshop in upstate New York. The piece is called "Casting" and recreates his experiences as a boy fishing with his dad:

Casting
Summer lay gently on the land that day, the lambent air, soft and warm, carried, for a moment, the voice of a summer thrush over the murmuring drone of honeybees. There was no wind this morning, all was motionless to suit the day. We parked and walked silently to the stream, lost in quite anticipation.

The water, over the tumbled rocks, gurgled with the unique sound of all shallow streams, a sound as ancient as the earth. We too, as fishermen, were of this brotherhood of ancient things. We assembled rods, strung the lines through the guides, attached the lures, and stepped into the water.

"I'll go up as far as the bridge," said my father, and smiled, because he would beat me to the first cast. And I saw the years fall form his shoulders. There was no gap between us now. We were both the same age. 🐟

CERTAINLY THIS BRIEF MEMOIR GIVES US IN ITS FORTY-FIVE seconds or so reciting time what a thirty-second commercial might give us. There is a specific setting established, images which set the tone of the experience and a theme briskly established—it too examines a particular moment when father and son come together in some timeless salute to love and companionship. The "visuals" are established early on and throughout the writing. Of course the power of the work comes through with the preciseness of the language, language that not only allows us to see the immediate setting but to place it within the spiritual human landscape which gives the fishing trip a universal nature, a connection to other men, other times—"a brother hood of ancient things." There is nothing, in fact, very abstract about this writing, and nothing vague. It is a tribute to our ability to sustain memories that not only distinguish our individual lives, but memories which define our magical abilities, our imagination and interpretive powers, to define moments by our emotional attachment to them. It is in all the multi-leveled association with the words we encounter, in fact, which not only suggest a timelessness by analysis of theme, but which alters even our time-frame regarding how we read and experience the memoir: although one could recite it in forty-five seconds, it takes much, much longer to "experience" the work—pauses, recollections, personal and universal allusions, reflection, and of course the standard of the quality of a literary experience, the urge to re-hear it or re-read it.

Ironically, the last two lines of the writing—"there was no gap between us now; we were both the same age,"—could easily be used as an effective "sound-bite" conclusion to some commercial promoting the product with appeals to succeeding generations, a car, clothing, cologne, exercise equipment, etc. But Joe Pohl's work gives those lines the context they deserve, articulating a particular thought that strikes all of us deeply as we remember our parents and hold them forever in a moment that defines a feeling that can't be duplicated by product endorsement. And that's the difference here between the million-dollar McDonalds ad where it is convenient to reach out for anything, even a Big Mac, to forget the fears and anxieties which are part of our home experience, and this seventy-some year-old man who has simply worked through his inner-resources to create a lasting memory of the bond that is suddenly illuminated on an afternoon spent fishing with his father. One avoids the story because it is overwhelmed by a musical phrase, the other invites analysis through its complimentary lyrical invitation.

The other day my nine year-old daughter brought a packet home from her third-grad class. It was a brochure, promotional letter and order form for something called Sentimental Souvenirs School Days Keepsake Collection of Memory Systems, a local business, as the letter explained, "specializing in the Packaging of Memories." Here's a part of the letter, addressed "Dear Parents," that was part of the package:

> These one of a kind keepsake systems are designed to be student friendly, allowing children from preschool through high school and even college to package their memories in a fun and organized way. Students have taken great pride in sorting and choosing their most treasure memories to preserve. What a wonderful way to encourage organizational and categorizing skills as they consolidate the "mounds of stuff" we all tend to collect into one compact place.

What was this "system?" It was a bunch of brightly colored three-ring notebooks and photo albums! That was it. The price? Well, of course, there were two, one retail, $59.95, and predictably the "special reduced price for student" of $49.95. This whole scam, this embarrassing ploy to conceal blatant consumerism with an artificial regard for education concerns, obviously was approved by both the principal of the school and the PTA (which is mentioned in the promotional material). I'm hoping a few teachers were outraged by this misguided promotion of cultural consumerism—but I'm not sure if any of them brought any of the issues so obvious here to the attention of their students (or if they were allowed to!). But the point should be clear: there was once a "compact place" (to quote Sentimental Souvenirs) where we decided not just what thoughts and experiences were memorable, but why experiences stayed with us were a joy to recall, or haunted us for that matter. That compact place used to be the mind, and its process became evident as we created meaningful essays, stories, journals or diaries, or even oral histories or anecdotes—and we could always keep a scrapbook, and you could get a photo album at K-Mart for five dollars and, with the encouragement of parents or teachers, decorate it yourself. This episode seemed so preposterous to me I couldn't believe it. Did any parents complain, send a note to school, or have a heart-to heart talk with their kids about it? I don't know. All I do know is that I couldn't have invented a more appropriate instance to make my point about how little effort we give the essential elements of storytelling and analysis in our culture compared to the degree and extent we push our young people into a culture of consumerism which eliminates inner-resources.

Let's pause for another commercial.

The most popular theme in today's world of corporate advertising is, aptly, gender hostility. Often, reflecting the confusion, resentment, and anger brewing between men and women concerning the abandonment of traditional roles that are at once romanticized and ridiculed in our society, often commercials promote reversal of gender roles. We now see the man on all fours in a garden, shirt off, smelling the flowers, while a woman looks on from an upstairs window, seductively fantasizing… and in one pants commercial, actually blowing the seeds of a dandelion she holds in her hand toward him. In another, it is the man pushing the shopping cart down the aisle in a toy store, the child tagging along, held in check from throwing teddy bears and things into the cart; and it is a man who comes across what used to be his toy, a full size Isuzu all packaged up on the shelf, and, of course, he too will have to ask mom, whose probably working in this inference, for the toy that was traditionally his to pick out and purchase—a sports utility vehicle at that! Certainly there is no denying the existence of genuine concern in both men and women when traditional roles are challenged, basically shattering the idea altogether of men being the bread-winners in the family and women being the stable homemakers that keep the destructive, dysfunctional forces of our culture at bay. There are genuine issues here that consciously and subconsciously need to be addressed—the socioeconomic reality is that, in real money terms, male earnings have been steadily declining over the past twenty years, probably as much as 20%. Woman, whether agreeable or not, have been forced out of the home for many years now, and, still underpaid and unemployed, find themselves slaves to male-created consumer images of them which promote, always, style not substance. There are serious questions to be asked; it is no wonder commercials promoting conflict between genders are edifying and engaging.

There was a popular General Motors commercial that aired over several months. It was an ad for a Chevrolet Camaro, and it centered on gender hostility, with a young free-spirited woman sailing down a country road on a beautiful summer afternoon. Camaro, it is said in the business, is a "woman's car," or a car appealing to young women in their initial new car-buying experiences. And how des GM relate to this important market group? Advertisers, in many ways more than literary artist, are sensitive and responsive to the emotional make-up of social and cultural issues. The intent of a commercial such as this one is to bring us immediately to the issue, allowing us to consciously and subconsciously recognize its relevance, and, crucial to the speed and intensity of the images that flash by us, lead us to the emotional reaction that allow us to vent without rational analysis. The woman is driving fast and seemingly carefree, at first resembling many car commercials of the past where the road (and the vehicle of course) is a symbol for freedom and adventure. But a few seconds into the ad we realize that there is much more to this than simple romantic flights of fancy. She begins shifting the gear stick, thrusting it with authority through the gears. Each time she does, with the Camaro roaring responsively in a deep-throated echo of words, she firmly declares the object of her wrath, the direction of her fury: "This," she declares, thrusting the consul shift into second or third, "is for my ex-boyfriend; and this," she continues throwing the shift forward as if she were delivering a knee to the groin of an intruder, "is for my boss… " This combination of wrath and freedom, harmoniously coming together with each verbal thrust, gives the car enough speed to pass a truck in front of her—and, as she does, we are given several angles of the event with a good look at the truck driver, a vile male with a perverse grin on his face. He looks at her and says something we can't make out, and then, disgusting as he is, points his hand ludely down at his crotch and says something to her as she passes. She's obviously the protagonist at that point, all the men in her life, including the truck driver, sharing the blame and being left behind. But we're not done yet. As she passes the truck, we see her coming toward us speeding down the road. She looks happy, thrilled really—as if anger and resentment were the culture's new highs; then, in a beautiful piece of camera work, she reaches up through her open sun roof and gestures to the truck driver she's left behind. Is she waving? We don't know because the shot of her hand is carefully blurred, a technique that's clever and effective because by this time our own subconscious interprets the gesture for us—the only gesture appropriate for this thirty-second adventure in hostility: she's throwing the guy a finger as she makes her way down the open road. This commercial too makes effective use of literary elements—the brief, immediate images and the indisputable tone of its human utterance, the clever variation of traditional symbols, and the elaboration of the open road metaphor. The viewer, once again, is edified, but, again, the issue is cleverly concealed—the product of corporate manipulators sensitive to universal needs but with no interest in understanding human predicaments. Their message: in the corporate world of General Motors, you can be delirious with revenge on others (and why shouldn't you be!), a trait not to be examined and resolved in some humanistic, empathy-producing manner, but one that makes you hip and cool as a consumer, a personal triumph that eliminates the need to see any further than gender hostility as an end in itself.

Compare the effective commercial with a similar theme in a brief story based on an oral history form an 80 year-old woman remembering her early life in America during the depression. Katheryn Edelman told this story as a member of our senior citizen oral history workshop in upstate New Your. We would hear the story as a group, probe for details, and I would transcribe it:

Convertible, 1928
Top down, eighty miles an hour, dust rising through the apple scented air of Route 104, little George strapped down to the brown leather cushions of the front seat, I aimed that Hudson toward Syracuse and pushed my foot to the floor...

I saw the car, white top up one day, down the next, in a showroom on Stone Street in Rochester. Everyday I walked by it, seeing myself behind the wheel, my sunlit hair in the wind.

When I told my husband I wanted it, he said simply, "Buy it," but he didn't say joyfully or eagerly. There was a kind of resignation in his voice; he had wanted to go back to Europe with the money we had—I'd wanted a house and that's what we bought a year earlier.

So I scraped up all the money I could get my hands on, abut twelve hundred dollars (including the mortgage money) and I drove that Hudson convertible right out of the showroom. When I drove it around the neighborhood, my friends thought I was a bootlegger's wife. I took weekly trips to my mother in Syracuse and I let the wind have its way with my hair.

But the broker didn't hesitate when our mortgage was late, and in thirty days past due there were locks on the doors, and the house my husband never wanted wasn't ours anymore. He got laid off too, being the Depression and all. Europe was even more distant in his eyes. So we made our way to my mom's farm in Syracuse, where we had to live for a while. Broke, we drove around in that Hudson convertible until even little George learned to laugh in the modest glory of the rumble seat. On Route 104 there were no speed laws, no cops, and we drove so stylishly fast, like a bootlegger and a bootlegger's wife. We were a little scared then, not of the speed, but because we didn't know exactly where we were going. &

(*story by Katheryn Edelman; transcribed and written by Ross Talarico*)

LIKE THE GM COMMERCIAL, THIS STORY TOO INVOLVES A WOMAN, a sense of frustration and impending freedom, and a brand new automobile. Of course, this rendering has something most commercials studiously avoid: context. The individual experience serves, as literature usually does, to illuminate a prevailing social milieu, in this case a predicament which comes into conflict with personal desires. The contrast allows us to see a vital

gap, in fact, between desire and reality, but it does so in a manner which gives us a fuller view of the range of human emotions—in this case, to use a phrase from Henry Miller, a kind of
"hopelessness without despair." Katheryn too is resentful of the
man in her life. He doesn't understand her needs, and wants to
retreat from it all. She, quite courageously and perhaps foolishly,
is obsessed by the symbol in America that represents, even in
1928, a spirit that would be impossible to suppress in a devastated economy: the new car and the open road, speed and freedom,
a new life waiting somewhere in the dusty unknown. But true to
the make-up of human complexity, fear is a part of the equa-
tion—without it the story of Katheryn would be merely quixotic,
foolish, sensational. We see the significance of the contrast
between the spirit of the individual and the drudgery of the
times. In the GM commercial the "victory" was superficial and
hollow, the possession of the car the only saving grace of an individual without any resilient resources; Katheryn Edelman's "victory" is qualified, as it should be, by the emerging awareness of
nothing less than her own humanity. The woman in the Camaro
throws a finger and there's nothing else to consider in a world
that eliminates reflection, analysis, and other possibilities.
Katheryn, on the other hand, understands the consequences of
her decisions, and delves deeper into her own resources, accept-
ing for a moment her ambiguous and paradoxical experience.
There is, after all, plenty to be angry and resentful about in
America in the nineteen twenties and thirties, people losing
everything and dreams dissolving in a disillusioned awakening of
social realities—there's no way to consider without some perspective of time and conditions which shape that individual. For
the woman in the GM commercial, the Camaro is *everything*; for
the storyteller in the narrative, the car is simply the vehicle
(excuse the pun) through which she recognizes the conflicts, the

cares and responsibilities (especially little George in the rumble seat), the vital capacities to worry, wonder, dream and survive.

Let make one thing clear. I am not writing to chastise the writers and producers of commercials! They do their jobs brilliantly. Their images are startling; their contextual brevity and economy of words is fascinating. They are lyrical, and masters at bridging the familiar with the unique. The point I want to make is that the intention of the commercial maker and literary writer is fundamentally different from the very beginning of the process. What I am concerned about is the idea that we are creating generations now who no longer can make a distinction between a brightly produced ad and an illuminating literary moment—between, in fact, a story and a non-story! In the 1990's, it is safe to say that the emergence of the sophisticated techniques of television commercials has influenced what we see in television programming, from sitcoms to news shows to MTV. Like the commercials I am reviewing, T.V. programming edifies us by bringing up topics that are, hopefully, of concerns to us, like the sitcom Friends (in a society where people tend to have fewer friends than ever), and Martin (where blacks have a wonderful sense of humor about their societal plight, and who are given a middle-class existence for their good sportsmanship), and MTV (where teenagers think they are seeing brief visual narratives to accompany the music instead of random images that serve to eliminate completely any sense of story whatsoever). Films, in turn, now strive to imitate its television counterparts since the audience has now been trained by television. In this steady bombardment, what is lost, of course, is the ability to even recognize what a "story" consists of—because the fundamental elements of storytelling are not really essential to our idea of entertainment. Reflection, paradox, recognizing conflict and ambiguity, compromise, and what T.S. Eliot called "the

contentment that comes with knowing there is no knowing"…
none of these literary components are desirable in the corporate
world of selling products—why would they be? It is time to edu-
cate ourselves, especially our educators and our children, to
know the difference, to make distinctions by being able to ana-
lyze intelligently what's given us, not just in the world of books
and literature, but in the world of "story-substitutes" that bom-
bard us daily. No, ad-makers, television producers, and blockbuster filmmakers do their job, and do it well. What we can't do
is ignore them, pretend that what they produce is not compet-
ing with the traditional sense of storytelling. What we need to
do is not look the other way, get snobbish or elitist about what's
happening to people young and old in America; what we have to
do is take a better look, a closer look, and tell our own stories
and refine them to establish an enriching norm. We have to
snap out of the half-daze that defines our passive yet receptive
response to television. We have to approach it with the same
critical tools that we use to assess literature and our own experiences. We have to "read" television. We have to "read" the ads
and commercials in America if we are to understand what is
vital and what is lacking in our culture.

LETS "READ" ANOTHER ONE.

Before I interpret a classic commercial from Coca Cola, I
should explain an essential concept to warrant off the typical
reply that there is no intended effort on the part of advertisers
to engage in the exploitation of prejudice, hatred, fear, etc. I
agree—no group of marketers sits in a back room somewhere
figuring out how to deceive the public or to take advantage of
the worst instincts in Americans. They do their best to simply
produce "what works;" and that's their job, without taking the
time or effort or money to articulate whatever themes may or

may not be inherent in their productions. A writer of literature, short stories or poems, or a storyteller in fact, would have that responsibility as a part of the genre or tradition. But commercial producers, those imaginative artists, are free to make their incessant pitches in a way that at once attracts an audience and keeps their product in the center of the commercial's consciousness. Next to the highlighting of the product itself, there really are no issues that require any serious thought, no human explorations required except for initial engagement. As a matter of fact, what they do consciously is make an effort to avoid presenting any real issue that might make the viewer look either beyond the commercial itself or, worse yet, inside him/herself to inner-resources which might provide the kind of nourishment that can substitute or even ridicule the consumer yearning for the product. So there is no secret committee, no darkened back room, and no cynical conspiracy—just a group of clever professionals engaged in a system that pays well and propagates itself. Since there is no story to be told, just random impressions, they just go about their jobs, not in a devious way, but seemingly immune to whatever interpretations may come from a more serious critical reading of their work.

The Coke ad begins with a black teenager getting on a bus in some urban setting. Several people get on with him and there are a few people sitting near the front of the bus, especially in those first seats that face the aisle. The teenager looks about seventeen I would say, and he's wearing headphones and carrying a walkman. As he gets on the bus, he gets a curious look from the bus driver, and as he begins to walk down the aisle, he gets looks of anxiety from a couple of people sitting in front of the bus, especially an older white woman. The young man himself is tall, good-looking, and light-skinned, and as the music increases in volume in the commercial, we see that he is singing along with that same music, which in the visual is apparently coming from the walkman and his earphones. So what we have so far is a variation of a stereotypical urban scene, one which is frightening to many Americans, especially white America: a black teenager getting on a bus in an urban setting. The looks of anxiety on the faces of those on the bus confirm this—an important image in the crux of the ongoing scenario. Should we be worried about black teenagers crossing the paths of little old white women in urban situations in America? In our stereotypical, prejudicial world, and in the context of both realities and myths about the violent, troublesome existence with young black men and boys in our inner city, the answer is yes, perhaps. And the commercial takes full account of that fear—indeed, it is the prelude to the commercial's real message which will follow in the next few seconds. As the young black man continues down the aisle to find a seat, we see the faces of the bus riders change from anxiety to a kind of simple minded cheer as the music swells and the volume of the young man's voice increases. We get a good look at him too—handsome, a voice like an angel, nothing in the least threatening about his demeanor. He is singing, aptly, the Coca Cola song, and by this point we are endeared by him, quite a contrast to the stereotypical reaction that caused the curious, anxious looks on others in the first place.

But the commercial saves its devastating message for the heavy-hitting conclusion. By the time he finds a seat, we are already convinced that he's an angel with a voice to match, and even the old white lady wouldn't have to worry if he carried her groceries home. But that's not enough as the commercial ends and we're singing along, feeling relieved and upbeat in a situation most suburban viewers wouldn't put themselves in for a hundred bucks. The last image is the *coup de grace*. Our final look at the young man as he sits in his seat reveals there is no

one behind him—for him to sit against the back of the bus
would be, no doubt, too blatant, might indeed startle us and
wake us from that half-daze so essential to television watching.
But he is, by all accounts and I'm sure not left to chance, the
black boy at the back of the bus—and the message is clear: in
the world of Coca Cola, in that corporate shelter where we can
feel safe, there's no need for anxiety because blacks, even
young, energetic black teenagers, take their place obediently
and harmlessly, where—in the back of the bus, of course, where
they belong!

In contrast, let's look at a memoir written by an eighteen year-
old black youth, Germone Wright, from a basketball/writing program in a community recreation center. It also takes place in an
urban setting, and it also has a gentle quality about it, and
though it lacks the catchy musical theme, the music of its words
gives us a deeper understanding of what it means to be a black
teenager in the midst of the inner city. Compare the difference
in the viewers/listener's reaction when you finish reading the
work: the concern is outward after the literary experience, a concern that is based on an awareness of context and social realities—the affirmation of human nature comes from a sudden
exposure to a world too often stereotyped and exploited, not
from a simplistic notion that we can shelter ourselves from such
exposure, denial, diversion, and corporate identity.

Father

On the corner of Seward and Jefferson, I met a bum who just
might be my father. At least he looked like the man I once knew.
At that moment memories came to my mind. I began daydream-
ing of the times he'd take me to the park. We'd go swimming,
and play tag until I was all worn out....

Suddenly I was back on Jefferson Avenue and all I saw was
the darker shadow of life. There were junkies and dope dealers

just standing around, all centered on the same thing, some dealers, some users. Then I thought to myself what did my father
do? He'd left so sudden I couldn't follow him. He left when I
was eight and now I'm eighteen.

 As I looked up at the sky, I saw only half the moon, looking
so dim. It looked like a light bulb about to blow. As I looked
down, the ground seemed broken up too, cracks in the street,
glass all over. As I looked up once more to look around, I could
not see my father, and I thought, there he goes again, disappearing, never telling me where he's going. ⟨⟩

SOMETHING SIMPLE HAPPENS WHEN WE HEAR OR READ A PIECE
of literature: we learn something. Sometimes it's a reiterance or
a clarification of what we already know or have suspected but
have not articulated in a meaningful way; sometimes the experience of the literature provides an insight, or another way of seeing or understanding; sometimes, in the works that strike us
deeply, we experience the epiphany that marks unforgettable
works. In this recollection by an eighteen year-old who, to my
knowledge, had never written much before, what comes clear to
me is the irony of the role reversal at the end of the story—the
son wondering and caring about where the father has gone, and
doing so in a "fatherly" way and with the maturity of a "father's"
voice. The story too, like the Coke ad does but in a more sophisticated, referential way, acknowledges the kind of things that
certainly make the inner city streets and corner no place to plan
a picnic. But it doesn't dismiss them or marginalize them in a
lyrical tribute to an illusory America where these things don't
exist. That's the difference between an ad and a genuine recollection such as this. In a brief story, which takes again in real
time no longer to read or hear then it takes to watch a commercial, we are taken through the complex mind-frame of a youth
recognizing someone who triggers a memory; we get the warmth

and intimacy of that memory, the sorrow of absence, and the sudden emptiness of a youth who has to painfully reverse the roles of boys and men. For me, it's a moving reminder of the deep psychological scars we have left on a nation on an entire group of children growing up and disadvantaged in urban America. It's not the Coke ad—and the difference is crucial: it brings us closer to reality, not further from it. We see the soul of a black teenager, not a light-skinned boy who, *believe it, can really sing!* (as might be the focus of the ad). One is the voice of our true humanity; the other is another version of MTV.

So what do we do? Of course one thing we can do—the focus of the rest of this book—is to learn how to tell and listen to and understand our own stories, and learn to identify their meanings. But there are other remedies. The fact is that we cannot pretend that television is just an innocent bad habit in a country where only the production of military arms is a bigger business then entertainment. Teachers across the country have to admit what they already know: little Johnny may or not may not read an assigned chapter any given evening, but he sure as hell will watch his favorite sitcom, and all the commercials which compliment it. No, we can't sit back and bemoan the diminishing reading, listening and critical thinking skills while someone making three times the pay of school teachers gets not only access each night to the young minds of America, but another million dollars or so in expenses to make sure the job is done effectively.

Before I make my radical suggestions regarding educators, television, and our youth in America, I think we should make a personal effort to incorporate storytelling into the ordinary routines of our lives. That, again, is what this book is all abut—how to tell your own story, how to listen and enjoy others' stories, how to share your lives and discover the meaning of the experiences that somehow stay with you. We must provide an alternative to the constant diet of media-hyped, product-oriented, simple-dimensioned and sensationalized productions that substitute for storytelling in today's world. Our efforts, in contrast, will be personal, honest, deep with humanity, and fraught with a genuine compulsion to carry on the species for the good of the species. It's that simple—and that vital. But to go forth with my suggestion for educators in America, to compliment our own efforts to reintroduce storytelling to our lives, here it is:

First of all, we should begin immediately to train our teachers in this country to develop skills in storytelling techniques and in critical analysis and apply those skills not only to literary experiences but also to television, advertising, and other media communications that produce the equivalent of and counterpart to the kind of reading traditionally assigned in our classrooms. This is no easy task. I am presently Professor of writing and communications at a university in California which certifies more teachers than any other university in the country; and I can assure you that analysis and interpretation of writing and literature, that critical-thinking itself, is not a skill generally nurtured or developed in our educators. One can't begin to "read" the sophisticated techniques of a big budget television commercial, for example, if one can't articulate the difference between subject matter and theme in a short poem, or recognize the inferred conflict or the prevailing metaphor in a short story. If we utilize literature—understand its component, its themes, and most of all its meanings in a social and cultural context so the whole process of learning is relative and sensible—then we can apply those analytical tools to the television equivalent of poems, stories, etc., that we're given daily as a cultural initiation into the world of consumerism. And that of course would comprise the next part of teacher training—to apply their critical-thinking skills to television, and, for a change, take the medium seriously and confront it head-on instead of dismissing it. For a start, I'd suggest that every new teacher trained in this country be given an emphasis, at least, in a cultural studies program in something that might be called Literary Media Analysis. I would suggest a course in Storytelling techniques and interpretation as well. At that point, I can make my most important suggestion:

That on any given school night, we as educators, send five or ten million students home with the assignment to turn on the T.V. and write a critical analysis of *Mad About You*, or *Home Improvement*, or *Friends...* or *Law and Order*, etc., and certainly a couple of major commercials that grace the "programming." Encourage the student to take a close look, a "reading" of the T.V. material as they would a poem or a short story. Indeed, a corresponding part of the educational experience would find works of literature that can be compared to the T.V. programming, and contrast them through critical analysis, much like the examples in this chapter.

Imagine the impact on television producers and advertising executives if suddenly they understand that educators fully acknowledge their extraordinary gifts in creating the equal of literature, programming that shapes the minds of our young people. They would be honored. And our children might begin to make a distinction between a "story," which is still the primary vehicle through which generations pass on wisdom, and a "non-story" (psuedo-narrative), where momentary sensations eliminate the need for a general perspective and provide for a parallel existence between isolated moments and isolated individuals.

Now let's get on with the essential purpose of this book, now that the "issue" of storytelling has a social and cultural context: telling our own stories.

THREE

Stories

THE FOLLOWING STORIES WERE TOLD BY ORDINARY PEOPLE WHO have never received or sought out training in writing or story-telling. Most had no formal training, in fact, beyond high school, and some did not finish high school. They simply joined a free, open-to-the public workshop I gave which motivated people to express themselves creatively. Of course everyone who joined shared something in common with all of us: when asked to remember something vivid in their lives, each had a story to tell; most had several stories to tell. The most immediate problem was "where do I begin?" The best advice I'd give was "close your eyes, and take a good look… "

Before we begin to discover how to tell our own stories, we should hear stories told by people like ourselves. Read them; read them aloud to yourself and read them to others. What you will experience is what I call the persuasion of primal narrative. What I mean by "primal narrative" is the establishment of a voice that utilizes qualities that are natural and universal to fundamental human expression. It is a voice that begins with the cave man grunting beside the shadows of his cave sketches, a voice which continues and discovers itself in Sir Kenneth C. Clark's articulate, elaborate explanation of "Civilization" in his popular PBS television series of the 70's. It is the voice of a grandparent, or a favorite aunt recalling old family stories; it is a voice that begins with a sense of urgency, but also a voice immersed in the calm of certainty and purpose. It is a voice substantiated by sensual knowledge, that wisdom we acquire through human touch and direct encounters. It reveals our curiosity, our empathetic need for each other, our quest for meaning in the onslaught of daily experiences. It is the voice that lingers when the subconscious demands assessment.

So whether you are the type to begin with a grunt (as I often do), or the type to begin with a keen observation (which I am known to do), the object is to simply "begin." These stories and commentaries that follow will initiate the fundamental first step of the process: *to reflect*. Unless you give yourself the peace and solitude of your own thoughts and memories, as well as those of others, you will not be able to focus. What you will discover is that the more engaging the story, the easier it will be to focus. What you will find also is that in the natural realm of primal narrative entertainment, clarity and meaning all go hand in hand.

The first story, "Silver Dollars, Silver Memories," was told by a woman in her seventies, Darlene Bargmann. I can't think of a better introductory story because Darlene's story compliments the previous chapter in the book by juxtaposing the literal value of the "silver dollars" with what they symbolically represent—in this case the objects that initiate the family stories at the heart of her fond recollections. In effect, it is a story about the importance of storytelling within a family.

Silver Dollars, Silver Memories

Every year when my mother had a child, my father gave her a silver dollar. So she had eight silver dollars. Can you believe that my entire childhood was spent borrowing these silver dollars and getting them back?

My mother was born in 1889 in Montana. My father was born ten years earlier than that in Michigan, and somehow made his way to Butte, Montana and married my mother. But there was no work in Montana, so my father went off to find work. "Go any place and I'll follow—any place but New York City," my mother said to my father as he left. So I'm here to tell you that he went right to New York City and found work as a barber! Mom arrived with us in a cold-water flat in Brooklyn. There was plumbing, but no hot water—just a coal stove in the kitchen where you could heat up water in the back. The tenement houses were usually about six stories high—and since the farther up the less expensive the flats, I want to tell you that we always lived on the top floor.

No, my mom didn't like it, but she knew she'd never have enough money to move back to Montana, so she said if she had to stay there, she'd make the best life she could. And she did. There were the days of large families, the days when moms were home. I remember how happy I was to climb the stairs past the floors of all the families—especially in the afternoons when all the cooking was being done. I can still remember the aroma of the pasta from the Italian family on the second floor, and the German sauerkraut on the third floor, and the sausage from the Polish family under us. We got along and there was a warm feeling of belonging that we all shared.

On the top floor, our flat, everyone crowded in on Saturday nights. We were not, let me tell you, a quiet family. My father played the mandolin, my brother Bob the guitar, Billy the banjo, and my brother Lou the saxophone. They would play and everyone would keep rhythm and sing along. I remember my mother putting pillows under our feet as we kept to the music, trying to keep the noise down. But there were times when neighbors tapped broom handles on the ceiling to complain. Funny, we didn't have much, but we were a together family, a loving family. No, my mother would never get back to Montana, but she left me the most wonderful inheritance I believe possible to bequeath a child—because she knew how to love, how to make you feel so good. She knew how to mother children… and I've certainly put that to good use in my life.

I was the last born, in 1930. I was the eighth silver dollar. My mother had a can, a coffee or cocoa can I believe. She didn't believe in banks (and we had nothing to keep in a bank!). And she'd hammer this can into the floor of the closet wherever we lived (and we moved often, let me tell you). In that can she kept the silver dollars my father gave her for each child that was born. I don't know how she thought that would keep the silver dollars from being stolen, but that was her idea. They were prized possessions. All of us knew how important these silver dollars were to her. She'd get out an old rag and polish them and then start to tell the stories behind them—who was there when the child was born, what the times were like, what the weather had been, if the child were early or late… I can't tell you the times Mama and Papa took out those silver dollars and the stories that would unfold when they began talking about them. As a matter of fact, the stories seemed to grow as the years went by—more and more details emerged; so I guess they were storytellers after all, just like I am now.

We were our own bank. We felt somehow we were rich with our silver dollars—eight silver dollars! When times would get rough, we'd take a silver dollar out of our "bank," the can in the closet, and we'd buy some groceries and tell the grocery man to save the silver dollar and we'd buy it back. I can't tell you how many times we brought back those silver dollars! Now, I'll tell you one story about those silver dollars. It was December. I was born in the middle of the depression, and I was about four or five, so it must have been around 1934. We had no money, and like others were having a tough time financially. My mother made many things we needed to live, including gifts for Christmas. But we were very poor that year. So we took a silver dollar to the grocery store and asked him to hold it and we'd buy it back.

He was a jolly old man, an Italian with a mustache and a big white apron and a straw hat, and he always did this willingly. In those times grocers and others had to create their own systems of credit and trust so everyone could survive. That was early December. We had another silver dollar out at the same time—with the man who sold the bags of coal we needed to warm the flat. On my way home form school one day, the grocer stopped me and said that if my mamma wanted that silver dollar, she'd better get him the money right away—"causa I a canta hold onto it mucha longer," he said in his thick Italian accent.

We took odd jobs and tried everything to earn money to buy back that silver dollar. We did mange to buy back the one form the coal man because we needed another bag of coal that cold December. But there was still this one silver dollar out. My mama said maybe we just had to let it go because she wanted us to have a little something for Christmas (she had been sewing for days). My mother, by the way, was the woman people called to help them when a baby was about to be born. She was popular because she had a hand-held scale. So if you didn't have mama there when you had your baby, you wouldn't know how much your baby weighed. You'd have to wrap up your baby and go to the grocery store. So mama was immensely popular. That December, the Italian family in the building called mama. They were a nice family, fun and warm, and of course didn't have much to give, like us.

Meanwhile we thought we had lost that silver dollar, and it was ruining our holiday. Every time I walked past the grocery store my heart was in my feet cause I felt so awful. It was

December 24th, Christmas Eve, and I'll never forget this. The Italian man whose baby my mother helped deliver gave my mother a box of chocolate cherries, and on the top of the box was a dollar bill!

Well, let me tell you, several of my brothers and sisters took that folded dollar bill and ran to the grocery store. The man was just about to close. When we walked in with the dollar bill he was happy to see us and gave us that silver dollar. And I'll never forget this: he wouldn't take the folding money, the dollar bill, and he handed it back to us and said, "Merry Christmas, children."

Time went on, and our family prospered, but my mother always had those silver dollars. As she got older, they meant a great deal to her. When she went into a nursing home, she had to take them with her, and, sad to say, I visited her one-day and someone had stolen five of her silver dollars. It was, oh my, such a terrible feeling. I bought five silver dollars and replaced them in the nursing home, and my mother never knew they were missing.

But I did take the ones that she still had from my father, and took the three coins to a jeweler and now have a beautiful long necklace with the three remaining silver dollars. But I certainly have those wonderful silver memories of my wonderful parents, and those stories they wove into my childhood that can never be lost and never be stolen—because they're a great inheritance. ᔆ

(story told by Darlene Bargmann; transcribed and written by Ross Talarico)

OBVIOUSLY, THIS IS A STORY ABOUT FAMILY LOVE, AN APPRECIATION of a time and circumstance that brought family members together, a recognition of a mother's care that the storyteller feels fortunate to relate. The storyteller's task is to find a way to make the abstraction of love (or any emotion) concrete (solidly grounded in a particular human experience). She accomplishes this by recreating all the details of her recollections—the consistent descriptions of the flat, the musical instruments, the odors of the food to suggest the diversity of life, etc. She creates the structure of the story (limiting the details by making the explanation of the existence of the silver dollars the center of the narrative) by use of the vehicle or direct subject matter (the silver dollars); the "incidental" or indirect information comes from her natural inclinations to make the story as vivid as possible, to include as many details as possible in order to make the reader or listener feel that he or she is there in time and place. Darlene doesn't summarize or give us an overview without first supplying us with fully detailed scenes and circumstances—one of the oldest maxims in creative writing or storytelling comes to mind: show, don't tell! The secret, it seems to me, since we can tell the "stories of moments" much, much easier than the stories of lives (that's what novelists tend to do, with great difficulty), is to choose very carefully the proper vehicle which will allow your story to initiate selective detailing and allow you to focus on a particular event, and "limit" yourself in order not to "ramble on" as your mind jumps from one event to another, which it naturally has a tendency to do.

Here's a suggestion: open a drawer. Choose a chest, a bureau, a desk—some place where you may keep some items that are valuable in the sense of being old, or passed down, or "special" in some regard. In it you may find an old scarf, a gold bracelet, a pocket watch, old letters or postcards, a ticket stub, a war medal, or typically, an old photograph… something that has a memory, a recollection, an occasion attached to it. Whatever the object, pick it up, hold it, look at it carefully. Keep it with you for a day or two, trying to recollect all the details that give the item not simply its significance (which the subconscious will always reveal as the details emerge), but more importantly its background, its setting, its physical context in time and place. You must fill in the very traditional blanks as would any writer—*where, when, who...* and these categories break down into even more detailed revelations, such as descriptions of weather, landscape, clothing, etc; or information about the specific time period of the recollection, such as the "Depression," or "after the war ended," or "when mom got sick," or when "the first television arrived at a neighbor's house." These kind of details will provide a historical or cultural context to go along with the physical context of the personal story you are creating. Keep a small writing pad with you and simply jot down any detail that comes to you—your subconscious will already be at work: trust it!

In Darlene's story, for example, the detail of the hand-held scale that her mother owned serves not only to give us a more vivid picture of her mother, and not only a deeper understanding of the economics realities of the age, and not only a vivid scene of the diversity that seemed to compliment community living at that particular time in our history—it importantly serves to provide the essential ingredient that allows the story of the loaned-out silver dollar to be resolved. To go a step further, though I caution this may be pure chance, the symbol of "the birth" at the end of Darlene's story leads to the fulfillment of spirit (it is true that our "symbols" come too from deep in our subconscious!)

I am struck, as I'm sure any reader is, by the loss of the silver dollars at the nursing home at the end of the story. That's the point where the theme makes itself perfectly clear: that the literal worth of the silver dollars can't be measured against the memories and emotions that they represent. A simple notion— but a notion that is meaningless unless beautifully rendered. I'm struck so much in fact by the story that I take it deep inside of me, as the famed psychologist Jung suggests to us in his well-known analysis of universalism: the story goes from an impact based on its individual or a unique quality to a universal feeling within that makes it every man or every woman's story. In the case of Darlene's story, because we understand at the core of our existence the struggle and love that tears at and keeps a family together, we are affected deeply by that ambiguity crucial to understanding the nature of our existence.

What happens next to me as Darlene's story has its effect is very common. It makes me think of loss, of family, of a particular moment in my own life that I am suddenly obligated to revisit—my own little story. And that's how good storytelling usually works: stories beget stories. It's as natural as getting hungry when the person next to me is eating a chocolate ice cream cone! Here's the moment that comes to mind.

I was first married while I was in graduate school at Syracuse University. Although I had a generous fellowship, we had no money, and my wife had to get a job as a nurse's aid at a hospital in the evenings. After our first year, which was spent in student housing, we looked for an apartment, and a friend and his wife were going away for the summer, and convinced us to sublet for three months. It was an old Victorian house, three stories, divided up into apartments, at one time an elegant mansion there on the south side of Syracuse where new shops were opening at the turn of the century. But now, there amidst the urban poverty of the 1970's, it was an anomaly, a Faulknerian reminder of a time long past, its presence an eerie testament to the deterioration of cities in America. We were young, romantic, and desperate for an apartment. About a month after we moved in, I left the apartment about eleven in the evening to pick up my wife at the hospital. When we got back, we found the doors busted open. The apartment was ransacked; the T.V. was missing, my typewriter, our checks, and some things form a small jewelry box on the dresser. In the corner of the kitchen, next to the back door, was a baseball bat with nails sticking out of it like spikes—the weapon of choice, we were told, for a bunch of drug-using thugs in the area. I was happy not to have arrived before they were through with their business. And everything stolen could be replaced. Except for one item, which makes the incident unforgettable.

Besides a few inexpensive earrings and bracelets in the jewelry box, there was one item, like the silver dollars in Darlene Bargmann's story, that had a value that could not be expressed in monetary terms. For our marriage, my mother gave me the diamond my father, who was deceased, gave to her some forty years earlier when they were married. It was a small diamond; my father worked in a shoe factory. But of course it was more valuable than any gem of any size could have been. It was gone. That empty feeling remains with me over the years. I have my dad's yellow Scripto mechanical pencil that he wore in his shirt pocket. I can light a cigar with his old lighter. But the diamond was special because it represented his love for my mother, his romantic side, his sacrifice in buying something that was beyond his means. In a sense, it represented my kinship to him since I was in a similar situation in my own life. No, it could never be replaced. Perhaps, if I added some details and developed the narrative, this incident might make a good "story," the kind that fills this book. But I didn't relate it here for that reason. I want instead to make this point; stories not only beget other stories; good stories told well often furnish us with insights into cultural matters. Let me explain in this case.

There was, I readily acknowledge, a sense of "romance" in the idea of moving into a house defined by age and character there in Syracuse. We overlooked the prevailing fact that it, like so many of the finely crafted structures of that time, was left in disrepair and abandonment, something quite common in a culture focused on seeking out the new, less complicated, more economical kinds of dwellings. The beautiful old houses became housing for the poor and disadvantaged in the core of cities, communities eventually riddled with crime and hardship. So our associations with "age" and "character," and even our associations with history itself, become either romanticized in some unrealistic manner, or become ingrained with hostile and fearful feelings directed toward social encumbrances—so much, in fact, that age and character are easily dismissed in a world of convenience and identities based on superficial appearances. Good personal stories give us a more telling account of our cultural biases and our state of being than news reports, statistics, or popular media accounts of our lives. We must tell our own stories, with details and accuracy, and with all the ambiguity necessary to define our complex character, if we truly wish to get a more legitimate view of who we are and where we come from.

MOST MEMORABLE STORIES ARE CENTERED IN A PROFOUND LOVE or a devastating death. The next story is a love story, one which lingers over many years, even though it is one, typically (if we are honest with ourselves), that never worked out. It is a story told by a black woman in her seventies, as part of a group that was encouraged to tell personal stories. " Train Ride" is surely an excursion through romance, an excursion across the country, and through our own sense of hope, infatuation, loneliness, and despair.

Train Ride
I. ATLANTA TO WYOMING
Choo, choo, clickety hiss… I'm on a train, heading west. He's a soldier in Wyoming, and he sounds as lonely as me. I read through another of his letters as the train thumps on.

Chattanooga, Sewanee, Clarksville, Paducah… the porter calls out. I keep his photo at my side, looking so tall in his uniform; I wonder what he'll think of me.

His name is Tommy Ross, and I found him listed in the Pittsburgh Courier, a colored paper we get in Atlanta. I just picked his name and wrote, and he wrote back. Six months of letters and then the invitation to the base in Wyoming. I took two weeks from the work I do, cook and nursemaid, and lately what seems just a sentimental fool. *Jonesboro, Red Bud, East St. Lou…* In the bag I packed I carry two dresses, always do, one black, just in case, and another the prettiest, prettiest blue. I carry a Bible, and read myself to hope and sleep. The porter brings some hot tea, no coloreds in the dining car. But there are stars galore in the western skies, and I pick one out and give it a wish, like everyone else traveling so far. I wonder what he'll think of me.

II. LARAMIE, WYOMING

Kansas City, Atchinson, Broadwater, Cheyenne… I'm coming just as fast, and just as slow as I can. *Choo, choo, chickety hiss…* I'm on this train, heading west. Before I know it, there he is. On the platform, so handsome, and even taller than his picture, taking my bag, my arm, and I'm still wondering what he thinks of me. At the barracks he drops off my things and shows me my letters in a duffel bag. At the cafe in the servicemen's club I meet a hundred soldiers, and they all call Mattie, like they've known me all the while. Turns out, Tommy Ross, he's got everything arranged—time off an apartment on base for the two of us, a dance arranged that night at the servicemen's club, and, after a night of holding me in his strong arms, an invitation to marry him that week. "You joking?" I say, and he just nods his head, and then I nod mine. The high altitude gives me a headache, and I think it's never going to leave, even as the chaplain is asking whether I do or whether I dare; and when I'm kissing Tommy Ross, and later dancing in his arms in my blue dress, and seeing the soldiers acting so crazy toasting us so on that joyful night, the headache stays, like a nagging memory, and all the happiness in the world can't shake it. When the two weeks is over he takes me back to the depot, and I close my eyes for a longer goodbye. Already the porter is calling out his song of destinations, *Northport, Gand Island, Boonville, St. Lou... Choo, choo, clickety hiss...* I'm on this train, heading east. We said soon we'd be together, but it wouldn't turn out that way. *Marion, Nashville, Chattanoo...* In Tennessee my head got better, but not my heart. I read through a batch of letters, and I looked at the photo that now would never do. *Choo, choo, clickety hiss...* I closed my eyes and remembered his kiss. I was a married woman, and yet, and how could it be: I still kept wondering what he thought of me.

III. GERMANY, FT. WORTH, TEXAS, AND ATLANTA

Six months later, without us ever visiting again, he was sent to Germany. The letters were slow, so slow I'd pray... There was so much, so little to say. I was a married woman, but no man around. I was a cook and a nursemaid and a sentimental fool. Again the photo was all I had; even Wyoming seemed like a cool mountain dream. For two years I waited for some kind of news, my heart full, the headache nagging with its memory. And before I knew it, the war was over; I got a letter from Oklahoma, and Tommy Ross saying he was being discharged, that he was going home, and to get on that train and meet him in Fort Worth in Texas. *Choo choo, clickety hiss...* I'm on this train again, heading west. Two bags this time, and just in case, two dresses, one black, the other the prettiest of blues. *Tuscaloosa,*

Biloxi, New Orleans, Port Arthur… I really didn't know what to do, apart so long, three years older, all that loneliness behind us. I was still a wondering what he thought of me.

And we were happy for a month or two. Conceived a child in fact. But it must have been bad blood, because one night it began to flow, and I guess it emptied both of us, and another night Tommy Ross didn't come home. And then another, and then one more. I could already hear the porter calling out in my mind: *Galveston, Baton Rouge…* And sure enough, a month later I was standing on the platform at the depot in Ft. Worth, the sky so dark and heavy, but me in my dress, the loneliest of blues. And on the train he sat with me a while, before the blast of the whistle and the *choo choo* and the *clickety hiss* of this old train heading back east… He said he didn't need nothing, and then he cried. He told the porter to take care of me, because I had just miscarried and was short of strength. When he left he stopped on the platform as the train began to move. He waved like he did in Wyoming, and I closed my eyes the same way. *Mobile, Georgiana, Tallapoosa, Atlanta…*

It's all a long journey, the one that leads home. I carried a bible, two dresses, a photo… I carried my love, whatever the pain, and when the porter says "heaven," and gives me his hand, I'll shake my head kindly, and tell him not yet, and I'll head on to Atlanta, where the sun starts to rise, where the light falls so briefly, oh Lord, and forms your beautiful tears in my eyes.

(story told by Mattie Whitley; transcribed and written by Ross Talarico)

WHAT WE SHOULD DISCOVER IN OUR ADULT LIFE AS THE YEARS and experiences pass by is that every "journey" outward is a potential vehicle for a corrclating "inner-journey," or self-aware-ness. The concept of a journey, in fact, is a traditional metaphor endemic to storytelling in general. Many people spend tremendous amounts of time and energy anticipating and planning for vacations not simply because the itinerary calls for such preparation, but because there is in the subconscious of individuals the exciting idea that previously undiscovered selves will emerge through journeys to "new territories." But the journey itself is never a simple, one-way effort. I have a creative writing exercise that I give my students in order to introduce this concept. I have them draw a line on a piece of paper. At one end I have them write the word destination, and on the other end the word past. They are told the line represents a road, or a path, or a river. And their journey on it represents the journey of life itself. Then I ask them to place arrows along the line—arrows pointing both ways, toward their destination and toward their past as well. I tell them that we constantly take a few steps backward if we are to go forward with a fuller understanding of not just who we are to begin with, but with why we're actually going where we're going. I have them make a list of what kind of things might both propel them forward and what might create intermittent retreats of some kind. So we begin to make a list—*curiosity, hope, imagination*, etc, on one side, *fear, reflection, security*, etc, on the other. It isn't long before we begin to understand the relevance of a phrase I introduced in a poem I published years ago—"the grace of hesitancy." We are hesitant at times because we are thoughtful, reflective, complex human beings and thus "journeys" are always fraught with the duality of going outward and inward at the same time.

But there are some other important instructions that go along with that same creative exercise. I ask the students to be as literal as they can be in their descriptions of the road, path, or river. I ask them to describe the roadside, each step, the riverbank, etc., as they make their way along the line. I remind them that the metaphor of the road needs a literal base, one filled with vivid, descriptive details, for it to emerge naturally, without the reader or listener feeling manipulated by some abstract and artificial concern with the sensual awareness that comes form literally being somewhere—that earthly existence from which most knowledge springs. It is, of course, a basic lesson about how effective metaphors emerge; it is a lesson storytellers and writers learn early.

The literal states Mattie Whitley passes through back and forth across the country reflect the many states of mind and emotional states that she passes through on this long journey to discover both love and loneliness. Stories that engage us often juxtapose strong emotional states, as if in that ambiguous experience we find ourselves balanced between desire and despair. In "Train Ride" we get to see glimpses of different settings, detailed moments that give us a sense of place, which, in turn, tend to highlight the sense of impermanence at the heart of Mattie's relationship with the soldier. The effect of the porter calling out the destinations, the names of cities along the routes, is also a part of the oral tradition—the lyrical naming of things, especially places,—as a means of giving the geography more of a human feel. Storytelling naturally incorporates poetic strategies. At the end of her story, when the porter holds out his hand and offers her "heaven," this strong woman stays in character and refuses. Although her stay fluctuates between romantic dreams and romantic illusions, by its conclusion we understand that strength in character often comes from emotional endurance. It took Mattie almost fifty years, as a matter of fact, before she told her story to a group of close friends—sort of like an odd model of a Polaroid camera, one whose negatives, when held to the light, take a half-century to fully develop.

IT IS A MISTAKE TO THINK THAT THE "MESSAGE" OR "MEANING" OF a story must be in the mind of the storyteller before he or she tells it. It is, very often, in the *telling* of the story that those things become, if not clear, at least more clear. In Harry Nollsch's story about growing up in South Dakota under the emerging shadows of Mt. Rushmore, an old man simply returns to a place he obviously loved as a boy. He reminisces in order to stay in touch with the reality of his early days, a life, perhaps, in contrast with the overwhelming dreams represented by the massive stone sculptures, heroes that reflect the "textbook" perception of American existence. For Harry, although this was not consciously in his mind when he told his story, his own experience on the wide-open range shaped his character the way the stonecutters shaped the portraits of the four Presidents.

Mount Rushmore

I can't begin to tell you how strange it is to see a face emerge, one feature at a time, from a distance only a young boy knows, there in South Dakota, in the thirties among the stretches of cropland, tied to the river of time by the brown waters of the irrigation ditch and good friends.

As an old man now I go back, visiting George, the other half of the graduation class of 1933 at the little country school we attended on the Western Plains. He now lives in the place my folks occupied when I left for the service in 1942. He takes me into the tiny room between the ice shed and the house where I slept as a kid, and he points to a dusty shelf, one I remember building over my bed more than fifty years ago. Still visible, the two hearts I carved there, one with an *H*, the other with an *E*…

I think back to Skyline Drive over looking Rapid City below me and the girl next to me in a '36 Plymouth; the lights seem to reach for miles. Even the glow of Ellsworth Air Force Base offers its promise of a country waiting. I look up to the darkness surrounding Mount Rushmore, thinking maybe the eyes of those four great men close at night, like ours, and maybe they too dream, like we do, of a vast country filled with adventure and love…

George tells me the young girl in my mind is now a great grandmother living in a town some thirty miles away. I wonder what we might say to each other, what anyone says really, after all these years. I remind George of the irrigation ditch, which would bring water to the fields of sugar beets, corn, and cucumbers, and where we'd go on those September evenings for a "last swim" of the season, the moon rising from behind the willow trees as we rode our horses out over the Dakota plains. The moonlight would dance on the little waves and miniature whirlpools in the dark brown water of the ditch, as we'd strip off our clothes and jump into the ditch, incredible happy.

I don't know, in fact, how my father managed those days; our farm was "dry," we had to rely on natural rainfall, my father forced to mortgage his livestock or farm machinery to tide us over until another harvest. How he ever fed us during those times I'll never know. As a matter of fact, gas always being in short supply, we only made it once to Mount Rushmore, seeing the faces of Washington and Jefferson, and the half-completed face of Roosevelt slowly emerging in the midst of such a barren and beautiful America. Lincoln's face, his stern resolve, was still a dream in the stone carver's strong hands. From that day on I took some time to stare out across the miles at those four men, and to meditate on my own achievements.

I run my weathered hand, still sensitive to the touch, over the initialed hearts in my old room, hardly big enough, I reflect, for a wish or two, let alone the contemplation of a lifetime, I know I'll never make it to the ditch again, and feel the cool life-giving water under the moonlight. But no matter where I stand, half of me in South Dakota, half in memory, I'm under the gaze of those four men atop Mount Rushmore, and I'll think about my own contribution to a life of hard work, decency, minor but wonderful adventures, and of course whatever romance one can find. And I'll stand back, the confidence only an old man knows, feeling that old September wind after a last swim as we rode our tired horses back home, that cold autumn wind, like a sculptor's hands, forming the expression on my face. ♫

(*story told by Harry Nollsch; transcribed and written by Ross Talarico*)

THIS IS A GOOD STORY WITH WHICH TO DISCUSS SYMBOLS. The fact is that symbols are everywhere! The trick is to recognize them as they emerge—as they naturally do. In Harry's story, the obvious symbol is Mount Rushmore itself, the massive stone of the American Presidents representing the strength and permanence and capacity of a country with unlimited land, resources, and potential. Ironically, the other "natural" symbol in the story is the irrigation ditch itself—not simply a means for enriching the land, but a place where the narrator and his friends, the working people at the heart of the claim to greatness, baptize themselves in a spiritual enrichment, something equally essential to the formation of character. His story takes a traditional symbol-the submergence into water as entrance to the subconscious—and gives it a fresh setting and an interesting twist: the young boys count on it to redeem the tough existence and barren landscape, but the narrator's father, we discover, does not have access to the irrigation. His father, in turn, represents the toughness in character that allows the monuments to emerge, no matter how difficult the circumstances. Along the way we discover romance, which always deepens the feeling for a place or a time; we also discover the inevitable exile, leaving home in order to "grow." Harry does what many of us feel compelled to do: he revisits home—physically, imaginatively, spiritually—and by giving us detailed accounts of a few experiences from those times, he gives us a view only he can give. He doesn't have to worry about a "message" or choosing symbols," etc. He simply tells his story with distinctive details, and the honesty and passion which gives his remembrance its inherent meaning.

ONE OF THE MOST DESTRUCTIVE EFFECTS ON TRADITIONAL narrative communication comes, oddly enough, from our culture's obsession with celebrities. We tune in our T.V.'s daily to find them monopolizing our talk shows, the center of attention on our "entertainment" shows, and popping up insistently on the news as well. Most of the time they have nothing to say except to reinforces the essential images of success, happiness, carefree living, hipsterism, and inclusion in a club that the viewers can utilize in a fantasy existence that keeps the real, character-building, self-reflective, socially-conscious stories at bay. Sadly, sports figures have been absorbed in to this category; subsequently, a vital group of men and women whose human feats traditionally paralleled the distinctive character at the heart of such achievements have almost disappeared in our culture. The star athlete's image is nurtured from the beginning by corporate endorsement marketing directors. So we end up with Shaq O'Neill, Ken Griffey, Jr., Michael Jordan, and Oscar de La Hoya—athletes whose inner-lives (and inner resources) are so concealed that they offer nothing to the viewer but the same bland, product-pleasing personalities that are completely divorced from the social and cultural forces that shape us, that especially shape the lives of their most ardent fans. The present craze with "reality shows" provides another example of the emerging gap between our passive worlds and the substitutes presented to us on television. Those shows create the impression that either our own experiences are insignificant or they are rendered insignificant because we have no forum with which to share them. Indeed, a culture bent on escapism does not need storytellers to remind us of who we are and where we come from and what we might require from ourselves to be independent of superficial concerns. So the Storytellers Slots in our culture—newspapers, T.V., radio (which holds on to a thread of narrative by the nature of its medium), role models, and even superhuman achievers—are filled with the wrong people: celebrities, sports figures, politicians, T.V. evangelists... a collective so out of touch with the enriching inner-resources of true character, that the slick, expensive ads and commercials that frame them seem a welcome substitute. To be succinct and to the point, we've created a sophisticated system that purposely obliterates narrative in our culture. It is no wonder that there is a ground swell of storytelling and story tellers in this country, and now there is a realization that if we don't make an effort to tell our own stories and learn how to listen and find the meaning of other's stories, we will give up our claim to creating our own sense of self, our own inner-resources, our own character based on strength and a healthy appetite for life, not escapism.

So I am pleased to share the following story with you. Johnny Antonelli was a famous baseball pitcher in the fifties and sixties, making All-Star teams and winning World Series games. He also signed one of the most lucrative rookie contracts ever (in real money terms) right out of high school in 1948. This is the story of how that all came about—but it is also a very human story about being poor, having good friends, a father who sacrificed for him, and, importantly, the sense of loneliness that he was faced with upon "making it," a loneliness, ironically, that, although often accompanying success in our contemporary culture, is usually never associated with it.

The Game
Of all the things to remember, I think of the cinders in my knees, sliding into second or home there in the field in the midst of the stored coal of the Gas and Electric lots at the bottom of

Ambrose Street. I'd wake Sal-Sal Magliosi, my best friend—
every morning by eight. Wake up let's go, the sun is up—and
we'd make our way to the coal field, where we'd choose up
among the six or seven of us and play ball all day, our bodies dark
with grime, but our hearts big and bright with each other.

Baseball came easy, but not life, there on the west side, where
money was tight. We moved to Ravina Street, and I remember
how difficult it was for my father to find work, but there was
always enough to eat, always heat in the house. My sister Lucy
held the house together, making meals and cleaning house, while
my mother worked. Anthony, my older brother, joined the Navy.

I kept playing baseball, loving the game and living the friends
the game provided: Joe Giardina, Joe Coccia, Babe and Carmen
Russo, Cosmo Trotto, and my new friends, Ray Quericia and of
course Gordan Scott, one of the only non-Italians to play ball
with us. At Jefferson High, in my freshman year, I insisted on
playing first base, wanting to play every day. But the coach,
Charlie O'Brien, saw the ball move when I threw it into home,
or around the infield. He saw, somehow, the spin, the "tail," the
natural curve, and that's when he said "Johnny, why don't you
pitch a little… "

I pitched, of course, and that part of my life is well known.
But while I was pitching, my father was cutting out the newspaper clippings and putting them in a scrapbook, and every spring
he'd go down to Florida, and hand out at the spring training
camps, and flash my clippings in front of managers and scouts
until they couldn't help but take a look. And then there was the
game that changed my life, here in Rochester, the night of the
25th of June, in 1948.

My father and a few others set up an exhibition game at Red
Wings Stadium. They arranged it so I would pitch for the
Rochester Stars, a local semi-pro team, against all-stars from

other teams in Rochester. I was a senior at Jefferson High School, and I had never pitched at Red Wing Stadium, never had pitched before a crowd like that, seven or eight thousand people showing up. Amazingly, my father had arranged for scouts from just about every major league team to show up at the game. And they were there, thirteen of them, to see me pitch! I pitched well the first innings, not allowing a hit, and the plan was for me to pitch just 3 innings; but the scouts pressed the manager of the Stars to let me pitch a couple more. At the end of the fifth, I was ready to give up the ball to the reliever who was all warmed up, but again the scouts prevailed, and I stood there on the mound that seemed so incredibly high on that stage, really, under the lights and applause from the people of this city, and I kept on pitching...

At eighteen years old we can do incredible things, our minds and bodies absorbing the energy from everyone and everything around us. At the end of seven I still had not allowed a hit, so the scouts and everyone else of course would not let me stop pitching. I had never pitched more than seven innings, but I felt a new strength, as if everything prior to this night had produced it, my love for the game, for my family, my friends. I pitched a no-hitter that night, all nine innings, and my life changed that night there, before the lights of my father's eyes.

Three days later I was given offers from every major league team. The owner of the Boston Braves came to my house. He was Italian, Lou Perini, an owner of a big construction company, and he and my father got along well. I signed with Boston on the 29th of June just three days after the game. My signing bonus was 52 thousand dollars, in 1948 quite a bit of money. The next day I packed my luggage and my father and I flew with Lou to Boston where that night we went to Braves Field to see my new team—in front of 30,000 people.

The next day my father flew back, and at eighteen, not feeling any pressure, no real decision it seems ever made on my part, I was given a room on Babcock Street, just a ten minute walk from the ball park, where I would throw batting practice and workout and observe the rest of the year. Suddenly I was on my own, a major league player, happy of course, but feeling a little alone, there, on the walk between Braves Field and the room on Babcock Street. It was a long way from the coalfield on Ambrose Street, but once in a while I'd find myself saying, as if suspended in time, wake up Sal, let's go, the sun is up. &

AGAIN, THERE REALLY IS NO NEED FOR COMMENTARY AFTER A well-told story. But this story has particular appeal for me because of our current reactions toward sports heroes. A couple of years ago, when I was involved in writing programs to motivate young people, especially our inner-city youth, I tried to contact several well-known sports figures and volunteered to transcribe some of the athlete's personal stories which might serve to motivate those young people in school and community programs. I thought, of course, that real, human, honest stories about the athletes' early years would create an empathy much deeper and universal than a sneaker commercial or a twinkle in the eye when shoving a fast food hamburger in their months. I not only volunteered my time, I volunteered a week-long writing program for teachers and students in the elementary or high school of their choice completely free, programs many schools now forego because of budget constraints. No one got back to me personally. The matter consistently went to the desks of agents, agents obviously too busy scheduling commission-based appearances in order to be concerned with literacy amidst the very youth which makes up a huge part of these athletes' dedicated fans. The result of "storytelling" falling into the hands of financiers and marketers: hero-worshipping without empathy—a formula completely antithetical to human understanding and self-reliance!

AT THE VERY END OF THE FOLLOWING STORY, BY EIGHTY-THREE-year-old Sarah McClellan, the storyteller says to us "One of these days you'll run into something that you'll be quiet about. And there'll be another day when all that silence will make you sing…" Wow! Forget about cultural interpreters like myself trying to articulate what's at the heart of this personal narrative business. Sarah captures it beautifully and succinctly.

Experiences that are truly meaningful and universal tend to render us silent. Sometimes it takes years for the scenario to come clear again in the storyteller's mind. And perhaps years later before the words appear. But the longer these moments go unexpressed, the more powerful they become when finally articulated. I think that's the case with this fine story about racial relations in the 1960's. The fact that a personal revelation tends to enlighten the reader to the social context of a particular time in America will be the focus of the commentary following the story.

My Certificate in Negro History

"You should have been there to see such a raggedy, hungry bunch, 1400 of us waiting in the rain and mud for a bag of yellow meal, lard and eggs, lines so long we'd have to camp out, or go back two or three days.

It was the freedom fighter, Pat, a sweet girl from Chicago, who asked me to write that letter to President Johnson when we was hungry and tired down in Cleveland, Mississippi in '66. We'd meet at the closed down Methodist school for a three day meeting, and Pat would give us some Negro history schooling, something which should have been ours all along. And in the evening too, in our little town, after picking cotton all day, I'd take my grandchildren, Curtis E. and Linda Pearl, and we'd meet under the good light of the moon, and in the deeper light of our eyes, there in the churchyard where Pat would show us photos and read to us about Negro sisters and brothers like Harriet Tubman, who done carried babies on her own back and drove stubborn women through the hills at night and into freedom tunnels of the underground railroad. My letter appeared in the evening news, and with it a hundred signatures from those who struggled to write out the proud letters of their names. Times were getting tense, oh Lord: you could feel it in the voice of the postmaster's wife when I went down to mail a letter and she'd ask if I knew where the girl from Chicago, the freedom fighter, was a-staying; the storekeeper would ask too, and so did the owner of the dry goods store. It seemed the more we knew, the quieter we were forced to become.

So we hid Pat from night to night in a different place—staying a while with the minister's wife, but even that wasn't safe. Just down the road in Mississippi we were told of the brush-hopper deaths, one little colored boy and two freedom fighters found dead (and decomposed) under a brush hopper in the sprawling, well-cared yard of a lady aristocrat who swore they were the remains of an old horse. And in Honanah there was going to be a march, and my son, Sammy Lewis, said Mama, don't go—and by the look in his eye I thought I'm old enough to mind my children, and sure enough, that's where Meredith was shot. And one day, someone said Sarah, the President sent us a plane full of food—he got your letter. So we made our way to the old schoolhouse, and we watched the county prisoners carry it in their gray and white stripes, big as my three fingers. Someone said the canned meat was ground-up cow hearts, but we didn't care, we were hungry. We waited in line for the coffee and yellow meal and grits. Some judges stood on the steps for a while and stared us down; then he sent a young white man down among us to take photographs of us. And someone else asked where Pat, the freedom fighter was at...

It was just the night before, in fact, that Pat handed me my certificate in Negro History, saying what a fine student I had been. "I don't want to go," she said, "but my time is up," and then she gave me a hug. Holding that certificate in my hand I knew that a person is a person, and out of one blood God created all nations... On our way home, my grandchildren and me struggled with our food cartons. The postmaster's wife stopped us and she asked, "Sarah, by the way, you know where that white girl is... "

I told my grandchildren then, like I'm telling you all now, one of these days you'll run into something that you'll be quiet about. And there'll be another day when all that silence will make you sing. 〜

(story told by Sara McClellan, transcribed and written by Ross Talarico)

I'M NOT SURE WHAT MY GENERATION, IN FACT, REMEMBERS ABOUT the civil rights struggles of the sixties and seventies. For the most part, I believe, there are vague, unresolved issues that fall into political or historical categories, but issues nevertheless that have not retained their compelling personal and humanistic powers. A well-told story humanizes a political or social force and individualizes it, until an entire movement both begins and ends with a singular human awareness, or a solitary life changed by a concrete understanding of the effect and consequences of human encounters. If this concerns older generations, then it is even more serious for younger generations, those whose sense of self might come from slick ads, media clichés, bombarded senses and discarded narratives. Sarah McClellan's story allows us to understand once more what civil rights was all about, reestablishing the personal issues of not just freedom, a complex concept that has become a necessary illusion for many of us, but issues of integrity, empathy between the races, respect, and hopefulness.

Through the details Sarah reveals in her pursuit of her certificate, we are suddenly privy to a time when hard work and a struggle for basic food and shelter did not dampen the desire, the mind's correlating hunger, for learning. This is really a story about pride and independence, people who, as Sarah tells us, "struggled to write out the proud letters of their names." It is also a story filled with *wisdom*, the word at the heart of storytelling, a word we'll be trying to define in the following chapter. Sarah knows, for example, when she's "old enough to mind her children," and, as Pat the Freedom Fighter hands her the certificate, she understands that the passing on of knowledge in this courageous communal endeavor is the spiritual moment that beckons God's universal blessing. I've made my living at universities associated with scholars and writers for many years, but I can say without hesitation I've never met anyone wiser than Sarah McClellan. In fact, it is that general wisdom, that ability to connect experience in its most elemental form, with a keen awareness of human nature that gives her a storyteller's power. When her story was published in the Gannett Newspaper in upstate New York she was given a special certificate from the New York State legislature. But the power of the storyteller goes much deeper to the soul of the community, deeper, in fact, than most politicians can ever imagine.

OF COURSE THE BEAUTY OF GOOD STORIES IS THAT THEY NEED NO commentary, no summary, no explanation or analysis, since they speak to an all-encompassing, intuitive intelligence that in turn informs our emotional and psychological selves… our whole being. So I'll share the last story of this chapter without commentary, except to say that when Rose Muscarella died, about a year after she told her story and I transcribed and wrote it, and after it appeared on the op-ed page of the Gannett Newspaper in Rochester, New York (and was shared by over one hundred and fifty thousand readers), I received a call from her relatives who asked me to deliver her story as an eulogy at the funeral mass. I did, as I have others in fact, and that moment seemed to touch those who knew Rose for almost ninety years of her life. They felt, in fact that it was her story that captured her essence. And that's just it: it is our individual stories, what we choose to remember, what we choose to cherish and tell (and the tone with which we express them) that gives each of us a truly singular existence. That's why human experience cannot regularly be mass-marketed in any richly fulfilling way.

The New Shoes

Funny how a life can change because you need a pair a shoes. It was the winter of 1921. I was twelve. My father died, just like that, leaving eight of us and my mother with not much except our love for each other. I remember how they lined us up there in the enormous room at Catholic Charities, where we went for shoes that snowy day. I was the oldest, and they lined us up by height, all the way down to my eight-month old baby sister in the arms of my mama. One by one, baby first, they brought us shoes, patent leather shoes, slippers for the babies, high tops for the rest of us. One of my sisters asked if it were Christmas, and it just as well might have been that year.

They gave my mom something too—a job. They arranged for her to wash floors for a hotel downtown. Now I had been in a "dunce" class, as we called it, at school, learning how to cook and make clothes and take care of the house. And suddenly, at twelve years old, that's what I was doing, quitting school and taking care of the family. One day I wrapped several of my younger brothers and sisters with warm clothes, and pushed the baby carriage a long, long way, all the way down South Avenue, to see the hotel where my mama worked. The babies were cold and tired, and I tried to quiet them down some when we entered the lobby.

We must have looked strange there amidst the grand splendor of the Hotel Bristol, holding hands and gathered around the baby carriage, dwarfed by stately columns and polished wood trimmings, while the suited bellboys and white-tied managers looked us over and spoke with their hands held close to their mouths. Then we looked over to the left and saw what we came to see.

There was Mama in her blue work dress, sitting halfway up the most elegant spiral, white marble staircase anyone could imagine. She was scrubbing the stairs with a rag, a bucket by her side. When she saw us, she waved, looking so tired and beautiful on that spiral staircase. I remember feeling hurt that afternoon, seeing her on her hands and knees washing the marble steps. The elegance of the staircase only emphasized the poor, insignificant figure upon it. We made our way home that day, a little exhausted by our trip. I got ready, and Mama came home as happy as ever. All of us were so close, like a stairway really, each year a step between us, each step a journey we all shared. I'm eighty-four years old now, and my steps are cautious and deliberate, steadied often by a cane. I walk painfully up stairs, but when I do I imagine I'm on the spiral staircase in the lobby of the Bristol Hotel. I keep imagining how elegant the rooms must be at the top of the stairs. And when I reach the last marble stair, it is my mother I discover scrubbing the final step, looking at me and dropping the rag into the bucket, rising to her feet and holding our her arm, which I take in mine… And together we walk down the steps, our new shoes gleaming, making our way home. *ॐ*

(story told by Rose Muscarella, transcribed and written by Ross Talarico)

FOUR

Wisdom and Community

THERE ARE TWO WORDS CRUCIAL TO THE UNDERSTANDING OF storytelling: **wisdom** and **community**. They are so crucial to the true nature of storytelling that we should repeat them, now, like a mantra of sorts, because they are the words most essential to understanding what this book is all about.

If we think about the words, we soon realize that of course they are related as well. The word that provides the essential bridge between them is "experience." Experience is a learning process; and in the experiential moment, someone learns something about himself or herself and the world. That is the illuminated moment, or the initial stage of awareness, insight, and knowledge. But it's not wisdom until the moment is processed—reflected upon, articulated, shared—until some sort of dialogue emerges and a perspective begins to form. In other words, wisdom is not endemic to a private encounter; it is dependent upon an exchange between at least two people, a dialogue, a give and take. Thus lies the magic of storytelling. Unlike the trend of "performance writers and storytellers" that have garnered public attention for the past decade or two, where the emphasis is strictly on gifted performers who simply entertain or amuse, unlike the impact of these stylized, solo, Hollywood-related acts, the magic of storytelling is that its true nature requires equally both givers and receivers, speakers and listeners—a "community" which can enlist and verify the "wisdom" at the heart of the shared expression.

In his novel *The Storyteller* by Spanish writer Mario Vargas Llosa, the narrator explains the incredible powers of a true *hablador*, or storyteller:

> Talking the way a storyteller talks means being able to feel and live in the very heart of that culture, means having penetrated its essence, reached the marrow of its history and mythology, given body to its taboos, images, ancestral desires and terrors. It means in the most profound way possible, a rooted Machiguenga (tribal native), one of the ancient lineage who... roamed the forest of my country, bringing and bearing away those tales, lies, fictions, gossip, and jokes that make a community of that people of scattered beings, keeping alive among them the feeling of oneness, of constituting something fraternal and solid.

KEEPING ALIVE AMONG THEM THE FEELING OF ONENESS, OF constituting something fraternal and solid! This passage from Vargas Llosa has to be one of the most thorough, insightful definitions of storytelling I have ever read. However, there is a larger point here that has to be made, and it is crucial to the theme of this personal guide to storytelling: the genuine *hablador* or *storyteller* in America as we reach the year 2000 is not the writer of sitcoms, is not the writer of television commercials, is not the harried newspaper journalist, is not the television reporter or a talk show host, is not the writer of blockbuster movies or the writer of comic books or the writer of fragmented thoughts inundating the world wide web. The genuine storyteller is, in fact, often not much of a writer at all, but someone wise with a material "feel" for narrative. This book is written with the dedicated belief that our most enriching identities will come from the expressions of ordinary people once we regain a belief in our expressive possibilities. As we reflect and focus on and become conscious of the meaning of our own stories, we shall "keep alive among us the feeling of oneness." Our stories will not be stilted by product enhancement, by promotion to celebrity status, by animated spectacle endings that serve to wipe out the inward exploration that makes us richly human instead of resource-less targets of commercial enterprises—a transformation that has turned the hunger for community into a hunger for consumerism.

Before we go on to create and develop our own stories, a step by step process that is designed to put yourself in touch with your deepest, most significant memories and with an objectivity which will bring out your most authentic selves, there are a few more ideas you should consider about the nature of storytelling, reasons why personal stories from ordinary people are essential for an enriched community.

We live, unfortunately, in a culture of alienation. Alienation is a fundamental experience of many Americans. The other day I walked through a stylish apartment complex in Del Mar, California. I couldn't help but peak through the vertical blinds of the endless rows of floor to ceiling sliding glass doors of each abode. In just about every apartment was a single man or a single woman sitting on a couch watching television. The televisions, it struck me, were huge, one bigger than the next—and then the equations struck me: the bigger the T.V. screen, the more lonely the person. We live isolated lives, cut off not only from others, but from our own feelings as well. The television, of course the most powerful symbol of our age, the single-most powerful instrument in fact that shapes our collective identity, provides us not only with a dizzying assortment of psuedo-stories, but with an ingenious, illusory receptor for our own vague concepts of who we really are. After all, would anyone choose to sit dazed and half-conscious, speechless and non-communicative in a healthy world of human species? The T.V. is, essentially, our community, something we can belong to, become intimate with, something which will allow us to come close to recognizing who we really are! But, of course, it is a false intimacy like the fraudulent schmooze of David Letterman, or the sentiment of the businessman calling home on the AT&T phone ads. And in the end, all our efforts to truly belong, to truly acknowledge our better, more communal, more charitable and social selves, collide with a greater force, the persuasive forces that make commodities out of our lives—or, to repeat myself, that turns *hunger for community into hunger for consumerism.*

The fact is, storytelling that makes a difference not only entertains, it provides us with a constant reappraisal of our potential for humanistic fulfillment. At the core of a good story is a feeling for life that cannot be communicated by simple information. In the Information Age, true narrative, the backbone of a good story, the element that connects the mind to the heart, that gives fact or fiction meaning, is hard to find. To create the reemergence of narrative, and to create again the kind of mind set to receive it, one must constantly question the kind of information we receive on a daily basis, information controlled, of course, by powerful sources whose main function—once again!—is to make commodities out of deeper, relatively unexplored communal desires. So the very nature of taking time to create a story or a memoir or an oral history, along with the ensuing efforts to reflect, recall detail, articulate conflict, rationalize choices, recognize resolution, etc… that process itself, in my opinion, constitutes a subversive stance in a culture where cliché, stereotype, random image, and convenience reign. It usually involves indirection, that is to say that the point of view, insight, values expressed, etc. are inferred rather than stated. Narrative, in fact, defies summary, paraphrase and all those shortcuts to interpretation. Indeed, that's what makes a good story more fulfilling than almost all other modes of direct commentary.

Let me mention more specifically four reasons why story-telling is essential in establishing the context where the self integrates with time, others, community, and the concept of being human.

1) Stories define *what is important to us*, what is essential for emotional and spiritual nourishment. A good story, and we can look at those stories that appear in the previous chapter for examples, leads us away from our worst indulgences, such as greed, alienation, suspicions and a consumer mind set, and leads us to desires more natural to our humanistic core—toward generosity, toward communal involvement, toward sympathy, and toward a spiritual need that comprises the life-affirmative quality of the story itself.

2) Stories are deeply rooted—not only in psychological pro-files and emotional expressions, but just as importantly they are deeply rooted in a sense of place. We cannot know ourselves unless we have a passionate understanding of the immediate landscape upon which human narration evolves. Basically, sto-ries help us recognize our kinship to the earth itself, elemental relationships between creature and environment. A knowledge of place is essential to a knowledge of self—the bond, in fact, between person and place determines not only a ways and means of living, river settings, mountain settings, lush land-scapes, urban landscapes, etc., but also values, imaginative visions, and a resolute fiber of character. Our oldest tales cer-

tainly, going back to our tribal existence, are predominately songs of journeys. Human awareness, indeed, has always been bound to a search for a harmonic relationship with the earth itself.

3) Perhaps the most significant claim I can make for storytelling is its *counter effect on the unfortunate evolving culture of alienation in this country*. For reasons I allude to in chapter two of this book, we have created a society made up of strangers; divisions between young and old, men and women, between races and classes, continue to multiply in America. The "harmony between person and place" which I mention above extends itself in a true story, since at the story's core is almost always a universal application of an affirmation of life; unlike corporate story-substitutes, a good story allows for the young to become old, men to become women, rich to become poor, and *vice versa*, and in the instant we cross even the smallest boundaries between us, an empathy evolves which directly confronts and challenges the forces of alienation that abound in our culture. *Good stories*, to change the famous line by Robert Frost, *make good neighbors*.

4) Finally, stories, by giving us an accounting of the past, provide us with a future of human possibilities. We learn, in effect, how to behave and how not too. In a culture brimming with an onslaught of information, with a literal smorgasbord of so-called available skills, stories allow us to make essential judgments about not just knowing how to do something, but judgments about *why we choose to do what we do!* That's the kind of judgment disappearing from our cultural agenda, especially from the educational experiences of students both young and old. Again, on our corporate system, a highly competitive work force focuses on how, not why! Knowing why we do something or refrain from doing it is tied, of course, to one of the words that begin this chapter: wisdom. Stories always teach us to question not

only our actions, but our motives as well. They show us the consequences of our actions, which is a prelude, of course, to understanding responsibility. Thus by making us more human, more whole in our self-evaluations, a good story makes us less prone to forces that divert our humanistic needs.

Another personal story
Here is another brief remembrance involving again my father and a holiday—this time Thanksgiving. It begins, though with a flash forward… to the time long past my father's death, when I am the father like him in the earlier recollections, in my forties, and, like him, trying to explain the unexplainable to my sons in that cycle of human encounters that is at the heart of the history of storytelling. Both these remembrances take place at one location, a grassy bank on Irondqoit Bay where my father, anything but an outdoorsman, magically pulled a bullhead trout out of the water with my bamboo pole when I was a boy. The instances, always current in my mind, are, in the world of time and circumstance, some thirty-five years apart:

… It seemed like the worst time of my life, my marriage to June breaking up—June, my friend and companion, my wife from the time we were barely adults, twenty-one or so—and it was without any doubt, my fault. Looking back, it was the worst time in my life as I would become another statistic in the quirky American culture of love songs and despair. I had moved out of the house, renting a small house, in fact, in the neighborhood where I grew up. Thinking back, that very gesture itself brought about a deeper, reflective state of mind—what had happened to that simpler life where relationships among family and friends preoccupied us rather than the isolated, illusory dreams that destroy the fundamental intimacy at the heart of contentment.

Thanksgiving was always my favorite holiday, a holiday that seemed to elude the commercial entrapments of Christmas. Having a meal together sitting at a table and having the time to look one another in the eye and speak cordially was such a simple, symbolic message for our culture. Our family always got together, my sister Judy and her kids coming in form New York City, my other sister Lonnie and her kids, my mother, and June and I and our two boys, Joey and Anton. I should have known there was something in the air this particular year when my sisters didn't invite me over to Lonnie's house the Wednesday night before. My sisters and I had always been close, and we had cherished our time together. June and I had planned on Thanksgiving at my sister's house, and that Thursday morning I arrived at our house to pick up June and the kids. My mother called while we were getting ready; she was crying as she spoke telling me that my sisters told her I was not invited for Thanksgiving, though June and the boys were. I called Lonnie to speak with her and Judy, completely devastated by their decision. Lonnie's husband Chuck picked up the phone and reaffirmed their decision, saying he did not want his kids (who were grown and to whom I was extremely close, their absolute "favorite uncle" over the years) exposed to the situation, although June and I were going as friends and family members.

It was Anton, my youngest son, eleven year-old at the time, who first spoke up. He would not go if I were not invited. Joey, my sixteen year-old son, quickly concurred. June, whose predicament was complex since she was in constant communication with my sisters since the separation, decided to go to the Thanksgiving dinner, and neither my sons nor I questioned her decision. Now I was already in deep despair over the separation, feeling guilt and blame, but this banishment from my family hit me hard. That afternoon my sons and I played a little basketball and watched football on T.V. My mother called from Lonnie's house, again in tears; apparently she sat there with her coat on asking others to take her home all afternoon. It was tougher on her than anyone.

About dusk I called a nearby restaurant and made our way to a place called The Bayview, a restaurant that sat along the banks of Irondequoit Bay. We ordered turkey dinners, and as I sat there I had to occasionally wipe tears from my eyes with a napkin. They were the kind of tears that come form the duality of the heart: tears of sadness, tears of joy. The separation from my sisters only highlighted the love and intimacy I shared with my sons. As I paid the bill, I glanced out the windows where the banks of the shore were lit with spotlights. It was then the image came to me, the memory.

Instead of walking to the car in the parking lot, I directed my sons to the shoreline. I then told them the story of my father on an afternoon in the summer about thirty-five years earlier, when I was about Anton's age. It was there, in fact, at the very spot we were standing that Thanksgiving night, where my father, in his clumsy but knowing way, put a worm on a hook on my bamboo pole and helped me toss the line into the bay water. I sat there holding the bamboo pole, waiting for something to happen. My father sat there smoking a cigarette, looking off into the distance as he did often, probably, as I thing back, thinking of another life, one where people gathered to discuss ideas and issues and the meaning of life, things not a part of the dialogue at the shoe factory or there in a relative's house where my uncles watched wrestling on T.V. He knew nothing about fishing. I saw him then as the father I knew, the kindest, warmest, smartest man I knew, one whose gentle intellect touched everyone around him—but I also saw, especially in the reflective years that followed, as a loner, a dreamer, a man whose ideas and insights were so private he must have felt that he was some-how in the wrong place at the wrong time—his grace served only by the enormous love he had for me, my sisters, and Gina, our mother. I pulled in the line and walked over to him. "Show me how, dad," I said, giving him the bamboo pole. My dad tossed his cigarette and took the fishing pole and stood up. He flicked his wrist and sent the line from the bamboo pole into the bay. Not thirty seconds later the line grew taut. My father, instinctively, pulled on the line and that's when I saw the fish actually jump out of the water, attached to the line. My father pulled the fish through he water and onto the bank of the shore. It was a good size bullhead, and my father had a big smile on his face. "That's how it's done, son," he laughed—and you know, I believed him; I believed, as I do to this day, that's exactly how it is done. Our small "miracles" come from the abiding presence of heart rather than skill. Later that evening, thirty-five years later, I sat on the couch with my arms around Joey and Anton, thinking how much my father would have loved them and they him (my dad died when I was eighteen, a couple of years older than Joey was on that night). I missed him. I missed my mom who was sitting there at Lonnie's on that Thanksgiving Day with her coat on and tears in her eyes seeing her kids divided for the first time in her life. I missed my sisters, and I missed June whose goodness shone like a star in the darkening skies of my own confusion. It was Thanksgiving, and despite the distances that grew like highways between our isolated, mortgaged houses, I sat there with my beautiful boys, thankful for what I had. 🍂

FIVE

Getting Started

WRITERS BLOCK! ALTHOUGH WE ARE OFTEN TOLD HOW TO AVOID it, the truth is that the strange reluctance we experience, that fear that fosters the seemingly irrevocable wedge between the compulsion to express and the words that make it possible, that condition is quite natural to anyone who feels the urge to tell a story. It is the distillation of experience, and we know, instinctively, there is a good chance that too many impurities—reality's never-ending onslaught of random details—will obscure the essence of the initial thought or emotion. My advice has been to attack the "block" itself by writing about it instead of yourself. Take the pressure off, in other words, and let the simplest words flow forth: *I cant' think of anything to write about… or, I'm not sure what was important about that particular day but I do remember… or, the only thing I can say for sure is that the screen door was ripped open that summer and the mosquitoes buzzed in my ear as I lay awake thinking about…*

The point is this: writers and storytellers know 1) that establishing a voice brings forth the story; 2) that seemingly unimportant details, once brought to mind or page by recollection, are the surest leads to what the story might be about (in other words, the story doesn't really exist until is expressed); and 3) that a good story emerges in terms you often cannot anticipate until you begin to recreate it. If you think of "writing to discover," you don't have to worry about "getting it right," a notion which paralyzes many beginners. I find that the easiest way to begin for most people is to focus on a particular moment—the day, the setting, the time of year, the weather, the color of the walls, etc.—and allow whatever details that might come forth to set both the tone and texture of the story. It might be a good idea to simply make a list of details surrounding time and place—what you see, hear, and touch as you imagine the reenactment. How many times does a sensory experience trigger a memory—for me, for example, the smell of lilacs (my first date, a disaster, with my first wife!), the musty odor of pillows (each day waiting for my parents to come home from work as I waited in my grandparents parlor), or the sight of an old hotel in a small town (dropping off a blind musician at a YMCA in a small town in upstate New York the day before Thanksgiving—and hearing him playing piano on the number one hit in America, *Midnight Train to Georgia*, as I drove off. A story I haven't finished yet!).

Think of the story as something unspeakable embedded in detail. It has no language of its own; it has no meaning or context of its own. The secret to its existence is that it cannot be extracted from the details that bind it. It is, in fact, the probe that gives it a physical presence—the way the body is the embodiment of the soul.

So Here Is an Exercise to Get Started:

Think of a particular day, a singular moment in your life. It might consist of a few minutes or perhaps a few hours. But it is the one instance, the one experience that you must try to recreate. Close your eyes. Picture yourself there. Alert yourself to the physical and sensual details surrounding you. Take your time—relax, take a deep breath, and realize that when your eyes close there is another world, one deeply embedded in your mind, that will become as vivid and as vibrant as anything you might see with your eyes open. Trust the darkness, it is where we dwell most of the time. Take a good look at the singular moment that you are recalling. Touch something in your vision. Smell the air. Listen.

What is the season?
Don't simply write down summer or fall, etc.—but write down the evidence of that season, the scent of the air, the frost on the window, the lace curtains blowing from the rush of stale air as the rusted fan groaned in the kitchen window…

What is the time of day?
Again, give evidence of the time, details, descriptions, not simply statements: the early morning sun danced on the brass photo frame, or, the darkness began to descend until the lone street lamp became the object of my contemplation… In other words, how do you know the time of day (without looking at a clock)?

You see something. What is it you see?

You hear something. What is it?

You touch something.

What every storyteller needs to establish is a **physical presence.** Before anything happens, before any moment transcends to an instance, an encounter, a conflict or an illuminating experience, the reader/listener needs to be there.

Physicality-details, descriptions, images—precedes the more abstract forces of a deeper recollection. Eventually, of course, your story will turn to what's going on in the mind of the narrator in that isolated moment he or she is recalling... but the trick is to get there as slowly as possible. Think of every memory as a photograph, a collage of related memories becoming a memoir. You have to create the photos with words. Once the images are clear, you can explore the complexities behind the images—until we see what the kitchen looks like, or who sits on the porch in the evening, or the family portrait, or notice what exactly is missing in the faded photograph... Until then, we cannot begin to unfold the intricacies of what makes a story ripen with age.

Once the initial portrait, that simpler moment which is the story's physical context is clear, then we can proceed to another kind of exposition, providing details that bring the story to another level of purpose. And what is the ultimate purpose? To recreate an experience that needs to be reconsidered, usually time and time again, because within its unfolding our humanistic potential is revealed.

But let's not jump ahead of ourselves. We're just getting started. Let's continue with the kind of questions that are basic to creating the setting, to creating the details that emerge from the subconscious.

When you list your answers—one word, a phrase, a sentence or two—to the questions posed earlier (*what season? what do you see?* etc.), write them down all over the page, staying away from our habit of putting them down in a linear fashion. Cover the page randomly with the details that comprise your answers—allow them the freedom of what seems like chance relationships; actually, something deeper and more mystical will eventually bring them together. It is our natural inclination to seek both order and meaning from the myriad of experiences that define our world.

There is a color that strikes you. Write down that color.

Blue
In the bag I packed two dresses, always do—one black, just in case, the other the pretties of blues... (from "Train Ride" p. 43)

Yellow
We were together that day, sitting in the tall yellowish grass of the orchard; I don't remember who took the photo, but we posed in the warm May sun, my cousin Dolores in her tailored red dress, blending in to the flowing meadow, her laughter catching the early wind of the season, so in love with her young sailor, Harold, who'd disappear some time later, lost overseas along with some of the joy Dolores would never again regain... (from "The Orchard Photograph" p. 82)

There is another sound. What is it?

Gunshot
Once in a while we heard a gunshot echo through the neighborhood. One of the troopers would shake his head, put on his hat, and walk down the driveway and look up and down the street... (from "The State Troopers" p. 148)

Piano keys
Even the black family next door came over to stay with us—they seemed more afraid than we were. Tillie was an entertainer, playing the piano for the rich in another part of the city. She

played for us one night; the troopers gathered around our piano, clapping their hands and singing with their huge voices. We all laughed so hard we forgot about the looting and the shootings, and the bad feelings and callused hands gripping rocks and sticks during the racial riots of 1964...
(from "The State Troopers")

You smell something. What is it?

Flowers—gladiolas
And a few months later, standing in the midst of such colors under the clear blue sky, I clipped those gladiolas, their scent rising from the huge meadow of perfume, each bouquet, hundreds of them, a strange blessing to a difficult life...
(from "Youth" p.132)

Food—sausage, sauerkraut
I can still remember the aroma of the pasta from the Italian family on the second floor, and the German sauerkraut on the third floor, and the sausage from the Polish family under us...
(from "Silver Dollars, Silver Memories" p. 34)

LET ME MAKE AN IMPORTANT SUGGESTION HERE: FOR NOW, JUST concentrate on the immediate descriptions—a phrase, or a brief sentence—as far as responding to those questions. The other details, the longer descriptions that will become longer sentences and more elaborate paragraphs, will come to you in time, and eventually you will feel compelled to write them down.

Let's continue with the random list of details. Fill your page with your responses: *A name comes to your mind* (as you imagine yourself in the particular time and place you are envisioning).

What is that name?

Another time and place comes back to you. Describe it. Who else is there? Describe that person or those people.

Write down another color. Describe what appears in your mind regarding that color.

How old are you in the scene you envision? What can you point to about yourself that is evidence of your age?

Do you like being that age at that time in your life? Why do you, or why don't you?

You hear someone say your name (literally at that moment or imaginatively in your mind). *Whose voice do you hear? What does the voice sound like?*

TAKE A LONG, QUIET MOMENT—ABOUT TWENTY MINUTES IN fact. Look at the words scribbled on the page. Say them over aloud—over and over until other details, other thoughts begin filling the silences. If you feel compelled to write down more words, or finish a sentence to elaborate on your responses, do so. But don't feel you have to. All that will come to you. But first you must open yourself to clarity—see more clearly, recollect with focus. You must begin to recreate and let the details speak to you. The story will come to you only when you ease your "grasp" of it.

As you begin to recreate the moment that requires reconsideration and illumination, you must understand that this particular experience you want to share with others needs a **background**—a background against which your story stands out. Thus, you must keep in mind that something unusual requires some understanding of the usual. Or that a deviant moment requires some knowledge of a moment that is routine. In other words, a good storyteller almost always has to communicate, even by inference, the norm against which a particular moment or instance assumes its specialness. So it is not uncommon for a storyteller to resort to phrases such as: *on any other day*... or *usually*... or, *it seems a little strange when*... or, in reflection, *but as I think back on it now*... These terms telegraph to a listener or reader a sense of distinction that marks every good story. I mention this minor narrative strategy here because as you begin to list the details and descriptions from your list and create sentences out of them, your subconscious will be whispering to you to remember how significant this particular story is. The same force that is feeding you details embedded in memory also is the force pressuring you to state the importance of the story. Don't state anything! Let me repeat that: **Don't state anything!**

The last thing a good storyteller does is often the first thing a poor (or "wannabe") storyteller does: make statements or pronouncements regarding either the importance or meaning of a story—and it's usually done before the story creates itself. The "wisdom" of storytelling is that it allows the listener/reader at least the impression that the importance or meaning of the story has been determined by the person listening to or reading it, by being told how to respond to it.

IN THAT SAME VEIN, THERE IS ANOTHER SHORTCUT INEXPERIENCED storyteller's resort to: summaries and overviews. Avoid them!

Instead, there is another strategy that writers and storytellers understand and practice: details beget details. Let me give you a couple of examples and then you can extend and elaborate upon the particulars of the scene you are recreating:

As you continue to reconstruct the scene from your memory, notice some objects around you—or on you, for that matter, and study them, think about them. There might be, for instance, a particular ring on your finger. Describe it. Where did it come from? What was the occasion upon receiving it?

You can do the same with any object—a bracelet, a vase, a trophy or a bookcase, a photo! Yes, photos, especially old photos, are germane to the recollections of stories. What particular occurrences or memories do they bring to mind? Who in a particular photograph is the center of your (narrator's) attention? Elaborate. By the time you choose several objects in the scenario you are creating for your story and elaborate on them, we will begin to see more clearly the tone (attitude) you will adopt toward the subject matter you are describing. More importantly, you will be creating the essential background, the context, your story requires.

HERE IS A BRIEF STORY TOLD BY A WOMAN IN HER SIXTIES BASED on looking at an old photo. Her name is Mary Wagner, and after she told her story I transcribed it and wrote it.

The Orchard Photograph
It's Spring. The perfumed blossoms held a flush of pink at their white centers, as if a velvet cheek, a sudden blush, could be seen showing through. We were together that day, sitting in the tall yellowish grass of the orchard. I don't remember who took the photo, but we posed in the warm May sun, my cousins, sisters and me, glad to be together. I remember Dolores most that day, her laughter catching the early wind of the season, so lovely in her tailored red dress, so in love with the young sailor, Harold, who would disappear some time later, lost overseas along with some of the joy Dolores would never regain.

To visit the country, my sisters and I chose floral dresses; we wanted to blend with the flowering meadows on the outskirts of Sodus. Under the blue sky, we took off our shoes and walked through the dry grass holding hands in a circle around Frances, my sister, who was sixteen that day, and blushing, like the pink at the center of the cherry blossom, when we sang out a rhyme about a girl's first kiss. Too soon we heard my aunt's voice; the birthday cake was ready, lit by the candles of a teenager's joy. But it was Dolores, more radiant than any flame, whose eyes filled with the sparkle of our own romantic notions, mentioning her sailor so often we felt his presence like a shadow lengthening in late afternoon. So we left the orchard, the serenity of a moment so brief and yet captured forever by a simple photograph.

I think of Dolores, her love defined by the years of misery and grief. And when I do, I feel the warmth of that spring day, the perfumed blossoms, the flush of pink at their white centers, as if a velvet cheek, a sudden blush could be seen showing through. ✍

(story told by Mary Wagner, transcribed and written by Ross Talarico)

YES, THIS IS A BRIEF STORY INSPIRED BY A SIMPLE PHOTOGRAPH. And it is the storyteller's cousin, Dolores, who obviously, stands out both in the photo and in her mind. It is not only the pleasant day in a meadow in upstate New York, the yellowish orchard grass and the red birthday dress—it is not only the happiness of the young girls that the storyteller captures in a brief moment. That context, the joy and innocence of youth is, in a subtle and natural way, juxtaposed to the story of her young sailor friend, and the barely-mentioned fact of the shadows of the war. It is, in fact, the juxtaposition of youth and innocence with that of the inferred story of Dolores' years of grief over the loss of her sailor that gives the story a depth that touches us in such a meaningful way. Of course we remember our own young, merry ways, our dreams, and the disillusions and disappointments that come with age and experience. Each of us knows about this process—and stories like Mary Wagner's remind us of this condition, this all too human blend of sadness and joy, that ambiguity at the heart of existence. All this from contemplating an object—in this case a photo, and within that photo the unspoken content. The simple object and the dynamic, multi-leveled, thought-provoking and poignant human interpretation: a story!

You can check the glossary at the conclusion of this book for terms essential to the storyteller's identity, but there are two terms that should be pointed out here, two terms which encompass both the complexity and whim of human existence: irony and ambiguity.

Irony generally denotes a discrepancy between the intended meaning of an event or situation and the real meaning. In other words, there is an element of surprise compared with the expected outcome of an event. The term is important to storytelling because it suggests that a meaningful story comes form a "new" or "enlightened" understanding of experience; it makes us reconsider human possibilities, and gives us insight into those possibilities—providing new depths of emotional interpretations. Basically, the term refers to our encounters with events that keep us on our toes, more alive to those moments which enable us to redefine who we are.

Ambiguity generally refers to the fact that a situation is expressed in such a way as to admit to more than one possible interpretation. Actually, such a possibility gives focus to two important facts essential to understanding the gist of a good story: 1) human nature allows us to experience several ideas and several emotions at one time (e.g. happy and sad, disappointed but relieved. etc.), and 2) a deeper inspection of a situation, based on a clear understanding of both context and individual, transforms ambiguity into a device to gain a more focused and clearer look at a particular moment. Like irony, it gives us depth and authority, and provides for more encompassing contexts and more thoughtful interpretations of experience. Ambiguity, subsequently, should not be confused with vagueness.

To conclude this chapter on "getting started," redo the exercise in which you respond to the questions about a particular experience of your choosing. Reread the brief examples here, and try to understand the concepts I review in this chapter, especially the terms I define, such as a writer's block, physical presence, deviant moment, summaries and overviews, unspoken content, irony and ambiguity. Then, pondering and expanding your list of details, write out at least a couple of paragraphs in which you reconstruct your "story," or at least a scene or event which might be a part of your story. After a day of contemplation, rewrite your paragraphs and expand if new details come to mind (they will!). Wait a day. Then rewrite it again. You are on your way!

SIX

Getting to the Next Level

STORY SUBSTITUTES ARE EVERYWHERE—HUMAN DRAMA AND explicit narratives have been replaced by celebrity worship (which allows us to forget our own lives), sensationalism (which overwhelms plot and the need for rational inquiry), and the laugh-track diversions of sit-coms (which edify us briefly but which ultimately conceal any human issue at the center of conflict). Our newspapers, for example, are filled with huge gaps regarding human-interest. We read about criminals, politicians, sports heroes, celebrities and victims, but usually we disassociate ourselves form those stories, making us feel even more isolated from events, more alienated in fact, because our concerns, our particular worries, dilemmas and joys are never addressed— it is a repetition of the effect of television on people: we are entertained, but feel left out, and the only way to feel a part of it, the commercials incessantly remind us, is to consume and become part of the consumer community, the new gauge of universalism in America.

What has changed, of course, is the perception of the purpose behind a story's existence. At the end of a wonderful movie called *Waterland* (based on the book by Graham Swift), Jeremy Irons, who plays a fired high school history teacher who can only engage his students by telling his personal and family histories, says during his farewell ceremony in the school auditorium that *when a child is frightened we tell him a story... to calm him.* He goes on to infer that storytelling is an assurance to frightened youngsters that others resolve their conflicts and fears no matter how dire a situation might seem. A "story" examines our vulnerabilities; it acknowledges our fragile but enduring humanity.

However, in a culture steeped in fears so deep they are suddenly beyond articulation or conscious acknowledgement, we become alienated from our own rational needs to come to terms with our vulnerable nature. So we close ourselves off, make ourselves non-receptive to a narrative whose nature is to enable us to open ourselves to a courageous exploration of experience. What is, then, a "story" to a person whose need to conceal overwhelms the urge to discover? In that world, the "story" is an outer garment—a material thing, style without substance, a fashion, and a disguise. The purpose changes. If indeed we are too afraid to be receptive to the consideration of an effort to calm, what then are we afraid of?

We are afraid, perhaps, that our own personal anxieties, our worries and fears, might reveal a weakness in character, open us to ridicule, to be—in the midst of a media culture ingrained with happy consumerism—labeled with a variety of derogatory terms, such as lacking confidence, failures, loser, "intellectuals," etc... We are afraid that our own very real sense of insecurity, once acknowledged, will isolate us, even alienate us from a culture where appearances determine status and introspection indicates suspicion. In other words, we might be afraid that a personal, dramatic inquiry into ourselves as we relate to the commercial version of the world that becomes our collective identity is, indeed, an indictment of character which will further alienate us from the world. We fear our "true" identity doesn't mesh with the "accepted" identities that our consumer culture promotes. The result is an atmosphere heavily polluted with negative feelings toward true dramatic revelation—an atmosphere receptive to a commercial bolstering of superficial rendering of character rather than one receptive to the revelatory elements of dramatic inquiry… or storytelling.

I think those fears are real and rampant. It is, if one can follow a logical and natural progression if these fears exist, that we are, in the absence of dramatic narrative, subject to the immediate impressions garnered through sensationalism, violent and sexual imagery, "special effects," stereotype reiterations, "victim" mentality, and appeals to defenses based on the concept of denial. This world hardly be the world where narrative could flourish, where drama could emerge, where "stories" could take on their traditional and fundamental place in society: to instruct, to create empathy and understanding, *to calm*.

What I propose is that we take something into our own hands. That we decide what's important in our lives based on human inquiry, on instinct, and a respect for an intergencrational, multi-diverse rendering of individual experiences. For every person struck silent and contemplative by the urge to tell in detail a story that has ingrained within him or her something valuable to relate about human existence, there are ten people making lots of money by generating story-substitutes.

One of the offshoots of this commercial endeavor to create story—substitutes is to create in our minds the myth of the significance of "celebrity revelations"—a tried and true commercial practice of validating experience through celebrities. In that world, changing a tire can be an affirmation of life because the mundane can be transformed into something magical in the context of fame, wealth, and power. Celebrities play an important role, in effect, in a world lacking the authority of storytellers, or in a world where people don't believe in their own abilities to convey significant information through the telling of a story. Here is an example—given through the medium which, I hope, best coveys not simply an incident, but the values and cultural assessment so vital to our real identity. It is another in the series of "father" stories that progress throughout this book.

Father

When I was a little boy, about twelve years old, one late summer afternoon in upstate New York, my father came home from working in the shoe factory and announced after dinner he and I would be driving to Alhardt's Appliances store a few blocks away. I couldn't understand why he'd want me to go with him to pick out a washing machine or a refrigerator. He then told me that he had learned that Otto Graham, quarterback of the great Cleveland Browns, my favorite football team, was there on a promotional tour, and that he, my dad, had been among the first ten people to sign up for the promotion, and for doing so I would receive an official National Football League football, signed by Otto Graham himself!

I could hardly eat my dinner that night. When we arrived at the store, wooden barricades marked off the street for about a block. There was a big hand-painted sign across the display windows which read *Alhardt's Welcomes Otto Graham*. I was surprised there weren't more people there, just a few anxious kids and their fathers and a few mothers and teenagers. There was a photographer from the newspaper, and there might have been, I don't remember, a local politician. No, there wasn't much fanfare at all. I waited in line with the other nine kids while Otto Graham, looking rather ordinary in his sport shirt, signed the footballs. In a scene that might have come straight from the T.V. series *The Wonder Years* a couple of decades later, when I told the great quarterback my name, he promptly signed the ball to

Russ instead of *Ross*—and then, before I could tell him that it was fine, that I'd simply change my name legally, he took the pen and tried to make the *u* into an *o* and suddenly the signature looked like one the neighborhood blowhard bully Kevin would have scratched on a cheap ball stolen form K-Mart.

The next part of the promotion, with the newspaper photographer snapping away, would also be unforgettable. Each of us kids that received the free signed footballs, one by one, ran down the middle of the blocked-off portion of Culver Road and Otto Graham, the most famous quarterback of our times there in the late fifties, threw each of us a pass. When it was my turn, I was as ready as I had ever been to impress old Otto, ready to show him the quick flank move that faked out so many of my neighborhood companions on the street in front of my house. I faked the cut to the inside and then quickly turned to my right with a couple of fleet steps and there was the football spinning in a perfect spiral from the fingertips of the greatest quarterback on this earth, falling right into my arms, perfectly thrown to the center of my chest and, incredibly, to my absolute horror, I dropped it. I picked up the ball, glanced down again at the screwed-up signature, and started walking over to my father who was standing on the curb, that wonderful, understanding smile always on his face. But—could it be?—when I glanced at Otto Graham with the sheepish look on my face, he motioned for me to toss him my ball again, and when I did he motioned for me to go long, to go out for another pass down Culver Road. I did—the straight fly pattern this time, to show him my speed, and wouldn't you know it, there again in the slow motion of that early twilight memory, the perfect spiral fell into the absolute center of my outstretched arms… Two perfectly thrown passes, two unbelievingly dropped balls! On the way home, my dad laughed in his warm-natured way, telling me not to worry about it. He said he was just happy to shake the quarterback's hand, and that I cold tell the story of playing catch with Otto Graham in the years to come. I took a look at the altered signature on the football; I could not imagine then that in a few years from that night my kids and I would have to pay for such an autograph. And it isn't just the humility of the dropped passes that has stayed with me all these years. It's how everything that night seemed to be connected on such an utterly and basic human level. Otto Graham, it seemed to all of us, could have been a next-door neighbor. He was civil, humble, kind, and what an arm! But what I remember most that night, oddly enough, is how the incredible kindness and love of my father gave the entire "celebrity" evening its meaning, even then. I liked Otto Graham because he blended so naturally with the adoring light shining form my father's eyes that night when he came home form the show factory and said, without a hint of the exhaustion or the frustration of working hard at a factory which gave him no pleasure in life, "Son, I've got a surprise for you… " ✍

I IMAGINE THIS STORY STAYS WITH ME BECAUSE OF THE NATURAL blend between an exciting moment and the loving milieu against which that moment plays out. In other words, it is the context which gives the story meaning. The contact with a "celebrity" heightens the awareness of the relationship with my father, of family life really, especially when we don't quite "measure up," which is part of the reality of life. How different that is from our obsessions with celebrities now—where they become the sole centers of attention, not to complete a context, but to divert us from a context. They have become, indeed, the substitutes for other role models in our society, and a diversion from an acceptance of being "ordinary." The point is simple: our personal stories help to define who we are by placing a moment in a perspective which more fully defines us as individuals, groups, races and classes as well. It establishes a sense of the universal, and, very importantly, allows us to relate to each other—not as "stars," but as fallible and empathetic human beings. Stories let us know who we are, not who we would like to be as representatives of a consumer culture, where wealth, material worth and fame becomes barometers of "success."

Our fear is the fear of exclusion. And that is the fear storytelling inherently tries to alleviate (... *keeping alive among them the feeling of oneness, of constituting something fraternal and solid.*) In our deepest human inquiries we are united. Here, then, is another approach to an exercise which might elicit a story from your conscious or subconscious state.

Exercise

There are few experiences endemic to everyone's life. Major instances which are surely democratic in their applications to all people are those which isolate moments that celebrate falling in love and moments that come to terms with the death of someone intimate. These are moments of course which deal with intensive explorations of both individuals and ourselves. A marriage, for example, celebrates not only the private love between two people, but an awareness that the world around us may be better accommodated by companionship, by an unselfishness that enhances life, and by the nurturing of an empathy that helps define the species itself. A funeral, on the other hand, brings us quite naturally to reflection to an assessment of human worth, to a recognition—again, of both others and ourselves—of the relationship between an individual and the world surrounding that person (How did he or she affect others—What legacy did he or she leave behind? Why did that particular life matter?)

Think back to one of these moments. Of course it isn't simply enough to merely "think" back; you have to let your thoughts settle into a time and place, allow the silences to linger, absorb the surroundings and go back to the sensual details of the moment itself—allowing yourself to see again the images of recreation. Perhaps it is your own moment—the day someone proposed marriage, or maybe it is your parents' story that must be retold in detail or lost forever. It may be the moment you saw someone you loved lifeless, the body so permanently at rest in a casket, the strange touch of the hand folded so unnaturally over the motionless chest. Surely that moment could be juxtaposed in a mind's instant to the hundreds of images of life flashing across your mind in the same instant.

What you should understand is that the very special moment—the kiss of the bride, the word "yes" joyously sputtered forth, or the kneeling by the casket, or the look into the peaceful face of a corpse—that these moments are simply the vehicles through which stories begin to be told. Those moments, as special as they might be, are, because of their universal nature, too difficult to recreate in a distinctive way. They can be, of course, culminating moments of emotion renderings—but they are dependant, as far as storytelling goes, upon their context—and that's where we encounter the true gist of the story itself—the anecdotal moment, the flashback, the illuminating recollection.

To begin, describe the day of the instance itself—not simply where or when, but descriptive, detailed evidence of where or when, so the reader can vicariously be there with you in your recreation. Pay close attention to the weather, the color of the sky, the smell of lilacs, exhaust fumes, a specific cologne, or bacon frying—any images and odors or textures which give life to your setting. Pay close attention to significant details, such as a description of a photo or a painting on a wall, a garment of clothing someone is wearing, something someone is holding routinely in his or her hands, a scar or a birthmark, a piece of furniture, a sound one can hear in the background or a popular song playing on the radio. There is no reason, as you describe the setting in order to allow the story to unfold, why you shouldn't include at least twenty significant details in the first two or three paragraphs of your remembrance.

If you begin with the specific moment of the declaration of love or with the first encounter with death, then your description should probably quickly turn to the transitional moment when your flashback or recollection can begin—you might use these common transitional methods/phrases—e.g.: *I remember how he used to be… or I remember the first time I saw him… or I can still see her on that warm afternoon in…* Remember, "love" usually allows us to see a world where its absence determines how we and others react to the meaning of love; "death," simply put, makes us reexamine life—again, lives of others and lives of ourselves. Your job as a storyteller in this exercise is not to tell the particulars of the moment of cognizant love or the moment of illuminating death but to fill in the gaps of the context during which these moments take place. In effect, you will create the whole picture of a small incident—that is the secret of not being overwhelmed by the enormities of the abstractions of love and death—terms that, in the end, contain only the meaning that the personal story itself ascribes to them.

After you write or record several recollections centering on an incident of love or death, share it with someone. Ask that person what else he or she might like to know about that particular experience. If you receive a response such as a "how did you feel?" remember it will do no good to try and describe *feelings*, which is every writer/storyteller's mistaken inclination (it's just too difficult)—it means, in effect, you have to provide more details about the experience, for it is in the details themselves that feelings emerge in the listener or reader's mind. Feelings are the unspoken mind-heart reactions to specific time-space objective renderings of human predicament. After you consult with your listener/reader—or if you use the group method where you share your early attempts with others in a fun but provoking gathering designed for social intercourse and personal expression (Storytelling Network Groups will be described in the next chapter), retell or rewrite your story adding new details and expanding the world of the "personal moment." As you do this, what you will notice is that the more personal you want the story to be, the more universal and socially encompassing the story will become. In the following three examples of ordinary people telling their stories, you will see nothing less than a time and place emerge, a mini-portrait not only of a person or people, but of America itself. The effect of a good story is that it defines us both as individuals and historic and cultural representatives as well. Storytellers emerge as the spokespeople of our times, thus ennobling what otherwise might be simply considered a personal indulgence. The following are some fine examples where the individual and the times come to light.

The Proposal
What I like is walking in the moonlight, listening to the echo of distant traffic, feeling my heart beat faster, and thinking it's great to be alive... 1925.

The Rialto Theatre on East Avenue. Sun shining on a Saturday afternoon, we walked from Bay Street and Eighth, my house, and halfway there, about two or three miles I guess, Joe put his arm around me. I'd known him about a year, but this was the first we were allowed to go somewhere by ourselves, just the two of us, though I had to be back by dark. We passed the beautiful lawns of East Avenue mansions, the museum and all its history inside the splendor of the George Eastman House, roses blooming along the trellis in the courtyard; and nearer downtown, Rueben's Furniture Store where we looked in and saw a beautiful polished maple dinning room set. And Hallman's Chevrolet, Joe's eyes gleaming like new paint; and the stately RG+E building. We watched the traffic, dreaming of our own adventures.

And after the movie, when Joe asked me to marry him, I heard the street whisper *yes, yes*. The blue sky too whispered *yes*. And of course I said it too.

(story told by Rose Muscarella; transcribed and written by Ross Talarico)

Rose's story give us not only a sense of her own excitement, but a sense of the times, how lives and modest American dreams (the dining room table, the new Chevrolet, etc.) came together in an urban setting in the twenties. In the next story, told by Texanna Sheppard, a woman a hundred and one years old, we discover a different kind of proposal, another kind of experience, this one rooted in rural life in the South in 1904.

Spring Vows
Down in Greenville eighty some years ago by the spring that ran through the Henson Plantation, I saw the preacher awaitin', leaning on the old bridge, and Robert in his clean new overalls giving him a dollar as the sun fell a little in that Alabama sky.

We had everything there, cotton, corn, cane and beets, but Robert had no family and I guess he wanted me. I was nineteen and he was older, forty-some I reckon, and he spent his days working the good road, six miles to a grader, twenty men to a mile. Some days he'd weigh cotton at the workhouse. But I guess he wanted me.

My aunt got our license in one of her trips to town. She was the only one to know. I told my ma I was going to wash out the clothes at the spring like always. I did not stay it was my marrying day. The preacher was in a hurry and didn't waste any words. We didn't even kiss when it was over, or should I say when it all began.

Robert went back to his place to gather collard greens, and said he'd come over in a day or two and tell my ma. I went home, feelin' good all over, and I was sweeping the backyard when I spied Robert making his way up to my mama who was sitting on the porch steps. "I come down to get my wife," he said. "You're not married," said Mama, kindly. "Yes dey is," said my aunt, peeking through the screen door.

It took about ten minutes to pack my bag. At Robert's place we stuffed the bed with cotton. We cooked fresh greens and after a while we gave each other a kiss or two. The moon shone over us and we sent out a little sigh to that Alabama sky. Robert held me so carefully, just like he was weighing cotton. And even the first night of our marriage we had everything we needed. ﾝ

(*story told by Texanna Sheppard; transcribed and written by Ross Talarico*)

IF THERE IS SOMETHING SIMPLE AND INNOCENT AT THE HEART OF these two stories, or something one might describe as civil, it is both a reflection of the times and a more forthright exploration of the inner resources which are fundamental to the concept of "love,"—a concept certainly challenged today as we apply a consumers' perspective to the idea of love and its overwhelming material context via commercial renderings of it. The next story goes a couple of steps further, capturing not just the early love—and the final love of endurance—but also the difficulties, both literally and symbolically, that give love its hard-earned role in human relationships.

Hands: A Love Story
My husband cut his hand in a machine that he thought he could run in the shop where he worked. He cut it bad enough—parts of a thumb and a finger cut right off—so he'd remember forever.

I remember that summer day in 1923, waiting for him to come home from the hospital, standing by the window looking out at Central Park, the grass so green and trimmed along the island between the streets, the maple trees fluttering their big leaves in the occasional breeze, and in the yards of my neighbors the lilacs opening in a blue and violet welcoming of summer.

I married Vince (we called him Jimmy) two years earlier and we were happy in those first years, putting our house together and Jimmy working hard so we could have the best of Sunday dinners. And we'd have three children before long, two boys and a girl to steady our love and help me through the days, the years Jimmy's mind started playing tricks on him, taking him away from us so often, so long, more than fifty years in the Veteran's Hospital in Canandaigua…

But that day, when I saw the "Garlic Flyer," the Central Park trolley filled with Italians with, as the joke went, garlic on their breath—when I saw the trolley I quickly made the bed, because Jimmy liked the house neat and he was coming home without part of his hand, and I rushed to please him so.

And when I finished, I happened to look at my hand—my wedding ring was gone, just a bare knuckle where the one-carat diamond had been. We looked all afternoon, and that night my father came over and we pulled the bedroom apart looking for the ring, but no one found it. It just vanished.

And it was never found; I remember missing it so, maybe not the same way Jimmy missed the ends of his finger and thumb, but I remember some fifty years later sitting at Jimmy's bedside at the VA hospital as my poor lost husband lay dying. I remember holding his hand that last afternoon of his life, and seeing his fingers that had been cut off so early in his days, and seeing my own finger so bare where the ring had never been replaced, and seeing our hands together, and knowing whatever was missing, the diamond, the flesh, had been replaced with care and love. We held tight, each heart giving a final squeeze, and then we let go, and all the pain and sorrow fell away from our hands until nothing seemed to be missing anymore. ⁂

(story told by Rose Venturelli; transcribed and written by Ross Talarico)

SOMETHING TO KEEP IN MIND: THE POIGNANT MOMENTS WILL emerge quite naturally in personal expressions that come from a single urge to express them. It is in the details, the descriptions, that need over-conscious attention. Why? Because they are a subconscious part of your recollection, already accounted for in the deep images of your own mind, but of course un-established in the minds of your listeners and readers. Rose Venturelli's story actually covers much, much more ground than I ever recommend to people. It is, as I have said over and over in this book, of no use to simply summarize a life or give an overview by itself. What Rose does in her natural ability to tell a story is to choose two or three very specific instances and describe them—the accident in which her husband lost part of his fingers, losing her new diamond wedding ring, and a visit to her husband's death bed in the VA hospital where he spent most of his adult years—and those particular images become very telling moments that are clearly representative of her life story. So even if her story covers many years, it focuses on specific times, very concrete details. The emotional impact of her story comes from the inference taken from her descriptive moments—she never really comments directly, you will notice, on her emotional reactions, and her story is stronger for it. Not being told directly how to feel, we have at least the sense of discovery by our own sensibilities and powers of intuitive empathy. Storytellers know there is no substitute for that. The point is clear: audiences are stronger when, as receptors, they gain a deeper faith in their own abilities to fully understand the overall implications of a story.

To end this chapter, I will tell another brief story regarding my father. It should be clear by now that I am purposely including a series of stories regarding my father. Since he died early in my life (I was eighteen, he was fifty-six), I imagine it has been important for me to recall memories of him since I realize he played so strong a role in my own understanding of the world. The story regards a funeral experience, to go along with the topics of the exercises in this chapter. However, this story, like many stories that stay with us for mysterious reasons, brings out the ambiguity that comes from trying to combine honesty and tradition. It is a story that might be offensive at first, certainly provocative. But, for me at least, it is a story that has helped me through the years to define the true concept of love.

Deaths

It seemed as if we had lots of chances to practice our grief. Once a month, or at least it seemed pretty frequently, we'd don our awkward black suits, usually bought in the budget section of Robert Hall's, and make our way to Falvo's or Profetta's funeral homes in early evening. It was mostly grandparents, uncles and aunts, or distant relatives, a family affair. But once in a while it was one of our own: Louie, the toughest guy in the neighborhood, shot through the head while deer hunting; Carl, running his car off a curve one fast night on King's Highway;

Larry, hit by a drunk driver as we walked home down Goodman Street after a minor fight at Skinny's.

In some of the funeral home visits, I remember thinking that emotion, at least the expression of it, could be induced by repeating faithfully a series of formal gestures. And, in effect, in some ways that was true. Even with the most remote of relatives, whose names I could hardly recall, tears would inevitably slip down my cheeks as I approached the casket, knelt upon the pew, made the sign of the cross, and glanced at the deceased with whatever compassion a frightened adolescent could muster in the midst of a grief I knew was waiting, if not there at that moment, surely somewhere down the line of my own life. More clearly, I remember a certain giddiness among my friends once we left a wake, even after the death of someone we were close to. We'd sneak off to a garage somewhere and sip some wine one of us had swiped from a pantry at home, and we'd get silly. I remember one Fall night after attending the wake of a girl on our street who died of cancer at eighteen, how we lit a pile of leaves and I think it was Mike who tossed a handful of bullets into the fire and we took turns darting past it while haphazardly, directionless, the little explosions rang out a last salute to our dead playmate.

Of course any psychologist could tell you that each awareness of death is really a reminder of life, however tentative, at the heart of each moment. We had, even then, as rambunctious teenagers, some vague notion of mortality; we knew that underneath the bravura, the cocky defiance, we were as vulnerable as the next guy, and that there would be a long series of little deaths to be experienced long before one could close his or her eyes forever. The trips to the wake were simply meditations.

Except for one—years before the others—which resulted in a strange and startling revelation. I was at the age of reason, seven I think. All night I kept hearing my aunts and uncles saying "Poor Sam, he's keeping it all inside… " Sam was my dad, and all the family and friends were attending the wake of my grandfather, my dad's dad, whom I knew well since he had lived next door. It was a typical, dramatic Italian affair, each relative carrying on with tears, gestures, and disbelief. All except my father that is—and so they assumed he was simply unable to find a way to express his feelings; and so did we.

Until we got home that evening. My father gathered my two older sisters and me around the kitchen table. He was honest, straightforward. He told us that as saddened as he was about his dad's death, he didn't seem to have any tears welled up inside him. As a matter of fact, if he felt anything, it was an emptiness inside. Finally, he looked at us and said that he didn't think that he loved his father, nor his mother, he added, who was still living next door to us at the time.

What a startling revelation for us. Imagine! A father telling you during those impressionistic years that loving your parents was optional. What a burden lifted from our little backs: if we were to love our parents (which we would do in great abundance), it wasn't because such love was obligatory, a duty, but because we chose to do so, freely and spiritedly. For some people I've known, the inability to come to honest terms with the relationships with parents has caused a lifetime of guilt and obsession. I'm thankful my dad tried to spare us of all that.

I think back now to those experiences, and give thanks… for those moments during which we were able to distinguish between legitimate grief and disappointment, which is everywhere. It was, of course, a prerequisite to knowing legitimate joy. ❧

SEVEN

Storytelling Networks: A Nationwide Linkage of Grass Roots Workshops

IMAGINE A NETWORK COMPOSED OF ORDINARY PEOPLE exchanging personal stories reflecting experiences that reveal our all too human existence. Imagine these groups meeting once a week, sharing these stories with each other, with other groups across town or across the state. Imagine these stories appearing in local newspapers, or local radio and television stations, being shared with school children as preludes to intergenerational classroom discussions, being presented in neighborhood newsletters or annual self-published books and presented in readings at libraries and community centers or in the council chambers of city halls. Imagine these stories crossing the barriers of class and race and age discrimination. Imagine them appearing on the Internet and becoming, for thousands of people across the country, the poignant and meaningful beginnings of dialogues which illuminate the human condition in the most tried and true tradition of our civilized lives. Imagine people once again wise and confident, and enjoying the company of others.

It's probably the curse of the storyteller in me! All my books, in fact, contain autobiographical data—even if I'm writing fiction or poetry. I make a quick, personal entrance, and sometimes just as quick an exit. A writer moves in and out of his material, testing it with his or her own character, substantiating it with personal experience, questioning it with the deep reserves of beliefs and curiosities. Yes, the storyteller wants to reaffirm the idea that what he or she chooses to remember and share indeed has meaning for others. So why do we live in a culture that is so alien to personal self-expression? Let me give you one answer. The need for self-expression is so deeply imbedded in us that it can be easily exploited by commercial merchants. We "express" ourselves in our society by the clothes we wear, the car we drive, the music we purchase, the sayings or logos that grace our T-shirts, the sneakers we wear. These are all, of course, commodity-driven identities, but they function as substitutes for the more personal expressions that may be hampered by complexities, such as—as I've mentioned specifically in this book—*paradox* or *ambiguity* or *irony*. So we simplify by adopting shortcuts to expression, based on marketing interpretations of the most general and stereotypical of experiences. It's good for the economy, and it spares us the "inconvenience" and "discomfort" of articulating our lives.

But it just doesn't satisfy us. Why? Because it's always someone else's story—and down deep, we know there's one of our own stories which makes the feeling more intense or the thought more clear.

I have spent a good portion of my life trying to make a case for the importance of encouraging people to express themselves and create at least mini-legacies of their own existence. Those efforts have led to some of the great moments of joy in my life: In 1994 I attended the premiere of the play *Hearts And Times* in Chicago, an adaptation of my book of personal narratives based on the oral histories of elderly Americans (*Hearts and Times: The Literature of Memory*), a play beautifully created and directed by Jackie Taylor, director of the Black Ensemble Theatre

Group. The music, splendidly written by Taylor and musician Jimmy Tillman, brought the words of ordinary people onto another glorious level of communication—and as I sat there on opening night, I could see in my mind myself at Kennedy Towers Residence in Rochester, New York, several women and a couple of men telling their stories while I sat there probing for details and taking extensive notes, trying to capture the distinct stories and voices of these people who simply had a story to tell. On either side of me, here and there that opening night in Chicago, were the "storytellers" whose stories filled the pages of *Hearts and Times,* and whose lives were now being played by actresses and actors before their very eyes. What a night—eight years of recording the stories of people, of finding numerous ways to share them with an entire city (Rochester, NY) through workshops, Gannett Newspapers, the ABC and CBS noon television news affiliates, through city-government sponsored readings and publications, through school districts, basketball-poetry programs to inner-city youth, through intergenerational programs which brought senior citizens and elementary school students together—from the simple sharing of experiences which did more to bring down the barriers between Black and White, Young and Old, Illiterate and Literate, Men and Women, Wealthy and Poor than any government-sponsored program I can think of. I remember walking the older storytellers to their bus that night (they had come to the premier through a city-government grant from Rochester) and standing there with my friend and publisher Tom Leavens I began weeping and couldn't stop. I was weeping because the wealth of our humanity had been tapped that night in the stories, faces, and good hearts of ordinary people. I thought that might be the beginning of an awareness of how important it was to capture our incredible individual abilities to not simply tell our own magical moments of experience, but to locate an audience which fully appreciated it all, an awareness of our own intimacies that allow us empathy, insight, and general respect that defies the forces of ignorance, prejudice, and artificially-induced hostilities between races, classes, and genders. The reviews were terrific. But the experience soon passed, a well-kept secret in a culture alien to the *community and wisdom* of storytelling.

I was, in fact, the only city-government sponsored, full-time Writer-in-Residence **ever** in this country. That glorious position, what I often refer to as "the best job in America," lasted for eight years—my job being to create events, workshops, relationships between the city and the school district, neighborhood programs and organizations and local media, all based in literacy, creative self-expression and storytelling as a means for community enrichment, all based on the lives and stories and creative efforts of citizens like you. That wonderful era in my life is documented in my last book, *Spreading The Word: Poetry And The Survival Of Community In America* (Duke University Press)—a book that was awarded The Mina P. Shaughnessy Prize form the Modern Language Association of America for the "outstanding book of the year on language, literature, and the teaching of writing." Of course I felt tremendous pride in receiving the prize at a ceremony in Washington, D.C. among thousands of scholars and professors, but despite the honor and the occasional note from the students or professors who have read and studied the book, the fact is the notion of a writer truly responsive to the community and in a position to share populist literature for the benefit of many rather than a few is still very much outside the framework of educational institutions and government entities.

I was thrilled to be named NBC's "Sportsman of the Week," spending a whole day filming with Katie Couric (who is sensitive to these issues) and appearing as a feature on The Today Show—for establishing a unique poetry/basketball program for inner-city kids in upstate New York, a program resulting in extraordinary writings from young people who wrote about their lives and shared their work and understood along with thousands of readers and viewers the universal significance of their unique articulations The day of my Today Show appearance I received a call from Stu Robinson of Paradigm Entertainment in Los Angeles. He viewed my work with inner city kids as "noble" and "inspired." He compared my work to the math teacher who inspired the film *Stand and Deliver*. Within a week I signed a contract with his entertainment agency, and in a month or so a few contacts with producers were generated. Stu called one night and said there was something brewing regarding a feature or made-for-t.v. film based on my work with literacy and poetry with young inner-city basketball-playing kids. At the last minute, Henry Winkler and his production company backed out of the deal. A couple of other producers remained interested. I kept wondering who might play me in a film—a daunting experience taxing my imagination in a bizarre fashion (I kept trying to think of someone who looked like a mix between Burt Reynolds and Woody Allen, two people I reminded others of!). One producer called me and queried me regarding a possible script. About ten minutes in to the conversation it was evident my life—all the incredible, joyous successes I had with black kids regarding literacy, poetry, community enrichment, and the obliteration of social barriers in the name of humanity... it was evident that these things just didn't cut it when it came down to choosing subject matter for prime-time television hours. It was a quick lesson in marketing sensibilities. I was told, for one thing, that married white females, who controlled the t.v. remote between the hours of 7 and 10 p.m., didn't really care about inspirational stories involving young black males in this county. I would somehow have to create a white female interest in the male character's life (me!); a rape scene would help out, or murder for that matter. There would have to be some kind of black-white tension in the story, and what kind of environment would be credible without some drug activity going on? Would I write a synopsis, enhancing my stories of blacks gaining self-esteem and empowerment with some dramatic content that might give a "story" more interest, more high concept?

What I'm telling you is simple. Don't expect our best interests as intelligent, thoughtful, and enriched representatives of the species to be the concern of any money-based, profit-producing institution that is tied to corporate enterprise in America. You might say I'm cynical. But that's not the point here. All I can tell you is that I encourage everyone to explore, define, and articulate his or her own thoughts and recollections of important experiences—as a matter of fact I've spent my life trying to do so. But so far the rewards are strictly personal—which may be, in the end, all there is. And yet without these personal, private rewards—those moments when you realize you have shared something from your life which someone deems meaningful—without those small moments of personal accomplishment, I shudder to think what else there is. I tell my college students who take my creative writing course to put effort and love into their work in my class, because it very well could be that they will never again in their lives be asked to express with any real concern, or with any serious audience, any articulation that encompasses a review of a self-expressive personal revelation.

And that's where the idea of forming a populist network of ordinary people telling their stories came from. No one else will do it for us—except for a book like this that provides some helpful strategies and some context to understand why and how storytelling fits or doesn't fit into our dubious cultural agenda—none of this can be packaged, or made generic, promoted as a money-making scheme or a self-help book that will "alter" your looks or financial status. Indeed, just the opposite: this book asks you to become more and more of the person you really are! If you feel alienated, which is of course a felling promoted by the corporate marketers of consumerism, a strategy to make you feel the need to change—or purchase—in order to feel included in a happy-faced, materialistic collective, this book is telling you that you have a right to be alienated because that's a positive sign that it is your personal experiences that are more real than the media is telling you about yourself everyday—and that your own stories are the sources of healthy identities in our world.

I'm sorry for the long prelude to this important chapter on forming our own Storytelling Network Groups. But you need to put your efforts into a sound cultural and social context in order for you to understand the meaning of telling your own stories and the significance of sharing them with others. You should also see, through my years of establishing groups of storytellers and writers, just how essential it is that *we rely on ourselves* to make sure our own lives are deemed meaningful and receive the respect they surely deserve.

Here's How to Get Started

All it takes initially is to get on the phone and call a few friends or acquaintances (or even relatives!). It's really nothing more than an ordinary coffee hour, a social gathering, but one in which each of you is going to share your own stories. Pick a particular morning and ask each participant to start recollecting details of specific memories from their lives. If you know the others well, you might even suggest certain instances that person might recollect. But remember, many great stories come from deep in the subconscious, because many are repressed, or so meaningful they're very difficult to express. So tell the other participants to come with an open mind too—and a notebook and pen to begin helping with notes, not only with their own stories, but to help details emerge in others' stories as well.

The size of your group can vary. I suggest to attain the balance between social gathering and storytelling workshops where individuals get enough attention without feeling too pressured, between four and eight participants. It can be all one gender. Some feel that all women or all men allow people to be more open or honest. I don't agree. I feel a mixed group of men and women, not necessarily equal numbers mind you, works much better, and in the end elicits much more openness and honesty. Sometimes, not all the time, it serves the group well for spouses not to be present.

Important!

On the day of the first meeting, don't think that suddenly people will open up and tell richly detailed stories that are succinct and economical, meaningful and focused! It's not going to happen. This book, in fact, takes on its indirect approach to storytelling—stories of others, concepts of storytelling, cultural agendas and story-substitutes-for a reason! Remember, this is a process—and it's going to take a little time for people to understand, for instance, that it is important to limit topics, to be as specific and descriptive as possible, to reserve overall summaries and editorial commentary, and to establish the habit of choosing and understanding the effect of selective details.

So for the first meeting or two, try reading other people's stories to each other—short, simple and un-intimidating stories such as the ones in the book. The most valuable lesson to be learned in the setting of the first couple of meetings is to establish the tone of the Storytelling workshop. The tone should be one of openness and honesty of course, but also understated, so "quiet" stories are encouraged more than "gag" stories or stories which end in a punch-line or a "surprise." The tone should probably be more melancholy than sensational, because at the heart of the personal story there tends to be a moment of awareness that reveals inner character—both distinctive and universal. Read these stories, others, discuss them, discuss how they might have been told, and then, casually, begin to allude to stories of your own—with each member of the group being alternative listeners, and probing genuinely, curiously, and imagistically for more details, to put the story in a more realized setting, and to get a better view of the characters involved, the situations, the times! For the first meeting or two, allow the workshop members to participate as naturally as possible, the most important encouragement being genuine curiosity and an interest in allowing others to develop their stories in ways which are non-inhibiting. Allow silence its own time and rhythm in your conversations. Careful words demand a certain amount of silence: we have to learn to be comfortable in its presence. Little by little people will open up and go deeper in their recollections. The group should simply ask for more details in order to create the images crucial to the story's existence. Again, try to discourage the use of summaries or overviews. Try to get the storyteller to replace generalities with specifics. Keep asking for more details. Get used to taking notes. Keep telling the stories over, and over, again.

Important Roles to Be Assigned in Storytelling Groups

Workshop Leader:
A workshop leader is more than just an organizer of the workshop itself. He or she, most importantly, must have a sensitivity

to the character or personality of each of the other members of the group. The workshop leader must sense a moment of urgency, a sudden compulsion on the part of others to sincerely express themselves. He or she has to make to make quick decisions on which stories at which time demand the attention of the group, and he or she must encourage that person without applying the kind of pressure that may cut the story short before it emerges fully from the subconscious of the storyteller. He or she must be *an outstanding listener*, leading the group as far as probing for details that will enrich the story being told. Everybody contributes as an enabler of others, but we often rely on one leader to manage the whole experience.

Transcriber:
Although all members of the workshop are encouraged to take notes a story unfolds, writing down details, specific phrases the storyteller uses, setting descriptions, and relevant additional details that may serve to enhance the final story, there will be one person who will emerge in the group as having a special talent in capturing the most essential, most lyrical, most symbolic and metaphorical details, and the person will become the "main writer" of the group who will be most helpful in putting together the final written product. Usually the transcriber will feel most at ease, sometimes from the simple fact of experience, with the language itself. Sometimes more than one transcriber will emerge, and that's fine.

Publications Manager:
This role is very basic, as much as a technician's role as anything. This is the person in charge of designing the page and printing up the material so it can be distributed and shared. It's fairly simple for the needs of the workshop itself. Just type it, make copies and distribute. But when the time comes for more

significant printings and distribution, someone well-versed in the art of publishing and printing will come in handy. For example, when a "piece" is submitted to the op-ed page of a newspaper, or to a local or community newsletter, or when something is printed for an intergenerational program for the school district, you will want a professional look, easy to read, attractive and without typos or other mistakes. It is an important job, even if you are preparing the stories from your group, you'll need someone who knows what he or she is doing, even if it's putting together the details of a contract with a local printer. In addition, you'll want someone to develop a web page, or someone who can open up discourse on the Internet for long distance involvement with other such Storytelling Network Groups, so you can connect community to community, city to city, state to state.

Additional Roles that May Develop Down the Road

Media and Newsletter Liaison:
This role may be somewhere down the road in your creation of a storytelling group, but it will be an extremely important job once the stories emerge and the time comes for sharing them with the community-at-large. In my programs as Writer-in-Residence in upstate New Your, the fact that I tapped the needs and interests of both major network affiliate news programs and the op-ed pages of the morning and evening newspapers gave our small groups of storytellers and writers audiences *up to one hundred and fifty thousands readers/viewers at any time on a regular basis.* I will give you several examples of op-ed columns that appeared in Rochester's local Gannet newspapers, all originating from storytelling groups. Interestingly, those individuals who told their stories and had them transcribed in our groups, were happy just to finally get them out, give them a voice after years

of simply letting dwell in a subconscious state, even if the audience were just several other people in the group. None of these people imagined that their own stories, no matter how brief or seemingly unimportant, would get the attention and respect of literally thousands of people at a time. Some of these stories were even translated into Russian and printed in Russian newspapers; some, as mentioned earlier, were adapted for the stage to rave reviews in Chicago.

The reason all this happened, and will happen again in communities across the nation once people begin forming Storytelling Network Groups, is because there is no substitute, despite the phony commercials, the insipid sit-coms, the sensationalized movies, MTV, dwindling vocabularies and attention spans, and a general lack of self-esteem that is the byproduct of alienation and a requirement for obsessive consumerism, for the individual human dramas that comprise our existence and that shape our true character which somehow remains *distinct, identifiable,* and *essential* to our human understanding. Someone from a recent storytelling group had these words printed across t-shirts that he passed out to others in the group: *Storytelling to Survive.*

Subsequently, the media and newspaper/newsletter liaison member of the story group will have to make contacts with local newspapers (especially for op-ed contributions), newsletters from businesses, neighborhood organizations, youth and senior citizens groups, etc., radio programs and local television, and offer human-interest projects (oral histories, memoirs, projects involving senior citizens and youth, etc.). But here is a warning: don't be premature with any offering. Don't offer an op-ed editor a story or a series of stories unless you have several polished, professional, "tested" stories at your group's disposal! Don't invite media to an intergenerational project involving senior citizens and youth and teachers unless you have some clear idea, usually by prior experience, of how the event will turn out. In other words, The Liaison Person will have to be knowledgeable and qualified to prepackage an offering to the media, keeping coverage of any kind focused with a direct and relatively simple effect as far as the news people are concerned; after all, they won't be interested in depth of character or survival questions. They are concerned with immediate effects, or how a "story" has an impact on the six o'clock viewer or the evening edition newspaper reader. In other words, you won't get a couple of chances once something flops: if the writing is bad, the event a "bummer," or the coverage a waste of time.

Let me share with you my method of sharing oral histories, stories or poems through a video presentation on the noon or six o'clock local television news programs. The oral history transcriptions and poems from youth in our community workshops were turning out so well, were so imagistically alive, lyrical and moving that I thought there might be a way to share them visually as well as literally with the television audience. I took a piece of writing, either a poem or a short narrative, and found a series of visuals that might illustrate it as it was read: the visuals comprised photographs from magazines and newspapers, mostly form the library archives—so if a personal narrative alluded to a time and place, even fifty years back or more, I could find illustrative visuals. I used photos, including old ones, that the individuals provided as well. The photo lab at City hall would re-photo the materials if needed. Then I would script the writing—simply marking off where each photo or print would be seen in the margins of the narrative or story. The TV. studio engineer would pick out background music (that would take just a few minutes) that was appropriate. Then the engineer would record me reading the piece. It is important in doing something like this to have someone with a strong reading voice record the narration. I can't emphasize this enough. It is much more important than having the original author or storyteller read the piece, although at times that may be affective. *It is important to hear every word, since it is the clarity of the story, word by word, which will carry the poignancy of the human expression.* Next, the engineer would splice together my voice reading the narrative slowly and clearly, the photographic images that were scripted to the narration, and the background music. The splices came together through fades, and the finished pieces, anywhere from forty-five seconds to a minute and a half, were professional, distinct, and I believe inspirational— television products from the simple stories of ordinary people. They were extremely effective and popular, and provided an excellent visual interlude between the four to six minute interviews, focusing on the enriching experience of community expression, that made up the news feature. It is an experience that can be replicated without substantial cost at any T.V. station in America. The television stations loved it, and the richness of the personal expressions encouraged more people to think about their own lives in a meaningful way. Of course, the videos could be shown in other places, in school rooms, neighborhood centers and to other storytelling groups.

School District and City Government Liaison:
This too is a role to be filled once the stories take on the format with which they can be shared and enjoyed. It is a role for someone with education sensibilities—knowing how students, especially young students, can be encouraged by exposing them to expressions and experiences from other generations, and *vice versa*. It is also a role for someone socially or even politically inclined, since the shared expressions of ordinary people, if they

are effective, bring many people together in the name of the *universal*. A good story often breaks down stereotypes and other barriers of prejudice and discrimination. There are great strides to be made involving school districts in the arena of community awareness and enrichment; it allows young people—as well as teachers and parents—a chance to see the relevance of communication skills, connecting, on a very basic level, human utterance with social predicament, personal expression with general sympathy, generation to generation, old to young, black to white, man to woman and woman to man. But let's not get too abstract. Good stories told or written well make for great schoolroom visits, neighborhood organization get-togethers, and city hall sponsored events that celebrate our common people.

Public Spokesman:

Although Storytelling Network Group members are spokesmen and spokeswomen for their times, and while the diversity of stories in a group or workshop adds to the ultimate identity of nothing less than our culture itself, there is always one person who can speak eloquently for public occasions. Once the stories develop, and once a community sees how enriched it can become by simply listening to its own constituency, the spokesperson might become very busy.

TO END THIS CHAPTER, HERE ARE A FEW EXAMPLES OF STORIES published on the Op-Ed page of Gannet Newspapers in Rochester, New York. The columns were featured on a regular basis while I oversaw the community storytelling/writing program, incorporating the stories and situations of common people into entertaining newspaper features. It is, I believe, the future of both journalism and local media engagement at a time when generic stories and Hollywood Hype seem to have no relevance to the lives of everyday people. I am, in fact, optimistic that once again our lives and our values and our sense of entertainment will find a common body of expression. And each of us will be the potential center of that healthy transformation.

The first newspaper column I'm sharing here I've alluded to earlier in this book—it has to do with poetry/basketball program, young people expressing themselves, and the tragic death of one of the young writers.

Chris Tuck's Quiet Vision of a Better Life Somewhere
I first met Chris Tuck at Flint Street Recreation Center in the spring of 1985. The basketball/poetry program was just beginning and I asked Chris if he would take part. I hoped he might become a model for the younger boys to emulate, not just on the basketball court, but as someone who might take time to express himself creatively on paper. He readily agreed, in his quiet manner. And later, as he sat there, his muscular body hunched over pen and paper, I thought again of an idea too often ignored: that imaginative thinking serves the same purpose as athletic activity—channeling excess energies into a healthful sense of well-being.

I knew, of course, that Chris wouldn't be any Shakespeare, but as I watched him staring into the blank page, I saw not just the athletic superstar, but a human being trying to utter a few words that might reveal a deeper identity. This was not a part of Chris that many people saw. One afternoon his mother came in to the recreation center looking for him. She was astonished to be told he was writing poetry in one of the back rooms. Indeed, that's where she found him, and that's where he wrote the poem that appears here.

Fast Break
When I let go
of the ball, I hear
the swish of the river
as it flows behind my back.
The stars and the moon stick
like knives in the mirror.
On a fast break I stumble
into the tall grass, and I hear my voice
getting shaky

CHRIS TUCK WAS ONE OF THE AREA'S MOST TALENTED BASKETBALL stars. Almost always described as a "man among boys," he led Charlotte High School to two state championships. He got in trouble for shoplifting and was suspended in his senior year. The brilliant basketball career everyone predicted never materialized, and Chris couldn't seem to avoid repeated encounters with the law. There were several charges pending against him when he was shot and killed in front of his home last week. No one who knew him seemed terribly surprised. He was 23.

Chris didn't stay long with the writing programs; he was moving too fast in other directions. Before long he'd find his way into tough crowds, courtrooms and even jail.

But when he took the time to write at Flint Street Center, and had his poem tacked up on the bulletin board there, he inspired some of the younger boys to take some time and express themselves with the written word. Those boys could never dunk a ball like Chris, but, like true competitors of a more universal kind, they could use their minds and imaginations to move toward better horizons. Chris, ironically, seemed glued to one spot.

When I read Chris's poem the first time I was taken immediately by the last lines: "I hear my voice getting shaky." It was, of course, a shaky time for Chris. He had no team to play for, no school to attend and so forth. Chris was often criticized for his toughness, his arrogance. I saw a more gentle side. He seemed sometimes almost apologetic for the immense physical strength that was his trademark.

Reflective moments—like writing a poem—bring out qualities that otherwise might go unacknowledged in someone (that is, in fact, one of the main purposes of community writing programs). When I look again at Chris's poem, as a critical reader might, I see that even at the moment of glory ("letting go of the ball") he imagines the "swish"—the sound of another environment ("the river flowing," and "stumbling into the tall grass")— which is curiously what many say Chris needed.

He tried playing ball at a college in Kansas, but that lasted only a few weeks. Brockport seemed okay for a short time, but he couldn't handle the academic work, and the old neighborhood kept drawing him back. I talked to my friend Gene Sullivan, basketball coach of Loyola University in Chicago, about taking Chris there, but that too was futile.

In his poem, even the stars and moon, objects that reflect someone's dreams and hopes, stick menacingly "like knives" in the self-reflecting images of the mirror. When dreams hurt a person, how far away is a tragic burst of that dream, or a shattering of an image?

It is no wonder Chris ended his "fast break" with a shaky voice. I get a little nervous too—seeing the life of a youth slip away like that, a young man who possessed so much God-given physical talent, the envy of so many. I think about all the young people without those physical talents, those "tickets" to whatever temporary fame people aspire.

And I think how so many will encounter the troubles of Chris Tuck, and how many will die tragic young deaths—and how their lives will not make the news, and how few others will ever know just how these young people existed. ᔥ

THE SECOND STORY CAME FROM A MEETING WITH A NEIGHBORHOOD committee that was trying to attain funding for neighborhood development. The committee began telling me stories of the history of its main street, Lyell Avenue, and the result was a humanistic approach to a political situation.

Lyell Avenue: A Neighborhood's Rich History Should Be Its Key to Its Future
It is 1928. The tulips surrounding Jones Park are blossoming, and younger Antonio, although he knows he should not, picks one for his sweetheart.

You can hear the saws going and the pounding of nails through the chill of the early morning air on Lyell Avenue. Peter Roncone is directing the carpenters, the German and Irish craftsmen who have built so much of the neighborhood. Peter is building a restaurant, a business he imagines that will provide his seven children with work in the years to come. You hear the bell and emerging out of what seems like nowhere, is the BLR trolley—an oversized train-trolley that turns onto the black cinder of Lyell Avenue from State Street. It will make its way down Lyell and keep going, the way you dream America itself just keeps going.

You step onto the trolley and before the first stop, the odor of fresh bread drifts over you. There is Rick Petrillo loading one of his horse-drawn carriages with stacks of warm Italian bread. Farther down the street, Father Ciaccia (some say the shrewdest financier in the city) is bending over next to a young boy, his hand on his shoulder. Behind him is St. Anthony's Church and School, an institution that embodied the first stages of the Italian immigrants who moved to Rochester in the early 1900's. The nuns who teach, work and live there, caretakers of the neighborhood, get $12 a month and room and board. Sister Angela waves to you as the trolley passes.

You pass the stately houses with the immaculate lawns and swept sidewalks. The grand porches will be filled with people tonight… every night. They are the recreation areas for people who know this is their territory, to build and maintain, to create a social atmosphere filled with laughter, discussions and respect. The two and a half-story houses, so beautifully crafted, illustrate the care of the immigrant tradesmen and their belief in a future far beyond their own lives. There is the Provenzano house, and you remember you must visit Mother Provenzano's general store on State Street, where she sells everything, including opera records, liquor abstracts, and multi-lingual newspapers. It is the store George Eastman visits everyday to buy a newspaper to bring back to his office across the street.

Lyell Avenue begins to fill up with people who are busy. The stately street might fool you for a moment, with its elegant houses and immaculate stores, but this is a working-class neighborhood, and everyone seems to have a job to do—which these people will do not as anyone else, but better, for they want the limelight to fall on them. Small businesses spring up everywhere—Cordaro's Meat Market on Jay Street, Borelli's Music Store, filled with pianos and the newest radios, and Scarfia's Grocery Supply, which distributes grapes each fall to the wine cellars of Rochesterians.

If you turn your head at the right angle, you can make out the wooden grandstands of Edgerton Park, where every fall the renowned Rochester Exposition and Horse Show is held, people from everywhere coming in their formal attire, pearled dresses and tuxedos, to see the finest horses in the country. And on Sundays, 25,000 people might show up to see the semi-pro football team, The Dutchtown Russers (named after the sausage market on Maple Street) play a team from Syracuse or Buffalo.

And as you turn your eyes back on Lyell, on the right you see a huge building jutting out on the corner, people going in and out at a slower pace, as if they had time to think about things. It is McSweeney's Hotel—400 beds for the poor, who are everywhere during the Depression. Leo McSweeney is the welfare commissioner, and the word is either he or the county owns this monstrous place (which would be called, ironically, Tent City, almost a half-century later), where someone out of work or on the skids could stay with meals for $ 5 a week. Farther down is Schutte's Ice Cream Parlor, where you can get a banana split for 15 cents. Lyell is an avenue for everyone, it strikes you, as the trolley makes its way past the No.5 Police Station.

There you see old cop Riley, just starting his beat, saying hello to just about everyone. He gestures with his white- gloved hands, a symbol, it might strike one, of a man who keeps law and order and makes no arrests. He is the one the young boys approach when they need a ball diamond to play on; he is the one who is told a family is hungry and the young father is thinking of stealing a crate of apples. He looks you in the eye when something needs to be settled, but makes you feel comfort, not fear.

On Avery Street, you see Asunta and John Cantosano tending the early tomato plants in their garden. In a couple of years they will have too many requests for Asunta's homemade sauce, and will begin bottling it in their three-car garage. It will be America's spaghetti sauce, and they will call it the name they have always called it; "Ragu!" And at the end of the city bus line, Burroughs Street, there's Joe Espositio's barber- shop, and Joe is already gesturing to his customers about some plan he has for the city. He will become the first barber turned county legislator, and his gestures will become the framework of public works.

The snow falls on the corner of Lyell and Mt. Read. Time goes on like the ghost of the old trolley, stopping along the way to drop off dreams and pick up hopes. It is 1992, December, and where apple orchards blossomed, the city's first shopping mall is as busy as ever. Men and women make their way to Delco and Kodak and a local judge can be seen making his way to Roncon's Restaurant on this Friday afternoon, making sure he gets a bowl of pasta-fagioli before it is gone.

If you listen carefully, though, you can hear the shovels of the Irishmen digging the canal; you can hear the hammers of the Germans building their boats on Canal Street. You can smell the fresh Italian bread of the bakeries. There is a heritage here, evident still as you travel the streets. You can see it continuing—by the African-American family of Taylor's Meat Market; in the Pakistani family who purchased Hericon Cleaners; the songs of the Hispanic children in Jones Park. The raw materials that made this neighborhood what it is are still here.

And you… slow down, let the years gather like a bouquet you're about to deliver, step off the trolley, take a walk down Lyell Avenue. The aroma of Asunta's sauce fills the air. So do the memories, the tradition. If the spirit is right, you can feel it; the old neighbors and the new taking the neighborhood forward. ❧

THE NEXT TWO STORIES COME STRAIGHT FROM STORYTELLING workshops, the first here, by Mary Verno, about growing up during the Depression near the train tracks.

Trains

The light of the kerosene lamp flooded the narrow stairway as we made our way to the unheated bedrooms, my two sisters and I sharing a double bed in one room, my three brothers sharing another.

We were tired and happy at the end of each evening, the heat from the potbellied stove downstairs we carried in our hearts, cuddling together, our dreams as warm as the oatmeal and hot cocoa that would await us in the morning. We ate together at the big wooden table in the corner of the kitchen. All the meals were prepared on the huge, black wood-burning stove, the loaves of bread, the heated kettles for our baths. We lived on the outskirts of Rochester, in the small town of Churchville. In our ample yard my parents planted a big vegetable garden, maintained several fruit trees and raised chickens. I remember the quarts of fruits and vegetables canned by my mother... where? On the black stove, which seemed to be the heart of our family, the source not only of heat, but of nourishment and companionship and meaningful chores.

All of us were lean and rugged, jumping rope and playing tag, surviving the childhood diseases, walking a mile to our school which housed all grades, everyone, from the first grade to the twelfth. I don't remember much about most subjects, but we learned the clichés, perhaps created them, such as "honesty is the best policy," and that "any job, no matter how humble, merited dignity and respect." There was something healthy about our lives in rural America, taking care of our selves, our needs, working hard, trusting others, content with so little, understanding our needs as simple, basic, communal.

One day as the sun began to sink into the warm twilight of the early summer sky, we were playing tag and munching on sweet red apples when it came down our street. We all stopped, our jaws dropped, eyes wide open, the apple cores dropping right out of our hands. We had heard they existed, but to see that first horseless carriage, that Model T Ford ride down our street with the strange couple dressed in suits and sitting so erect and floating effortlessly through the sudden landscape of our dreams, to see it must have changed us in some way, because I could feel the desire, right then and there, to travel, to go elsewhere, since there was a big country out there just waiting for us.

And sure enough, my father needed a job only "the city" could provide, and that's where we went, where my father found work as a plumber's helper, and where we found a small house in a poor neighborhood near Bullshead, where the lawns were neatly tended, and the sidewalks shoveled clean in winter. Our house faced an empty lot, and on the other side of the lot ran the railroad tracks, where the freight trains would pass several times a day. I remember sitting there on the front steps as the train rambled past. The freight trains carried all kinds of goods, and I can still smell the odor of the pigs as they passed squealing, the faint smell of oil from the tankers.

We imagined the sacks of flour and corn there behind the doors of the closed cars of the long freighters, cars form every corner of America, the *Santa Fe*, the *Baltimore and Ohio, The New York Central...* But just as we imagined all these goods filling the warehouses and stores of a country blossoming with dreams and opportunities, with something incredibly abundant for each and every one of us; just as we imagined our homes filled with everything a child of America could desire, a freight car would pass with a door way open, and sitting there, swinging their legs and looking so lost in their huge coats and baggy pants, the hobos would pass, our eyes meeting theirs, their bodies as lean and rugged as ours, and sometimes we'd wave, not knowing of course that all of us were heading for a similar destinations.

When the Depression hit, my father lost his job, and my mother took in work from a local button factory, and all the older children helped sew buttons on cards. Some of us harvested crops on nearby farms, and my older brothers worked as caddies at a golf course in a plush country club, where life somehow went on in some strange leisurely way that didn't make sense. We pooled our money, but there was never quite enough, and during the winter months we ended up on welfare, though we kept it a secret, thinking it was a disgrace. During those times we lived on homemade pasta, combined with beans or lentils, and tomato sauce. For lunches, there were large skillets of fried potatoes and bowls of lentil soup, augmented by thick slices of my mother's delicious bread. We were, of course, lean and fit, as we were meant to be, walking everywhere, somehow happy as a family, hopeful and amazingly in love with our neighborhood.

And before long, the freight trains chugged past regularly again, this time carrying tanks, and jeeps, and in the shadowed doorways where the hobos had ridden through the heart of our country, rode the soldiers with their lit cigarettes, their innocent grins, and their waves that seemed to say too many times, good-bye. We waved back, tears in my mother's eyes as my brother too left for the war. We have all worked hard, most staying lean and trim, though a little less rugged as the years have been good to us. The other day I found myself telling one of these stories to my grandchildren, who sometimes, I know, find things difficult to imagine.

I wish I could gather them around the potbellied stove so they too can feel that special warmth. I wish I could light the stairway with the kerosene lamp and flood the hallway with light so we could see each other for both what we were and what we have become. ❧

THE LAST STORY IS BY MATTIE WHITLEY, THE WOMAN WHO TOLD the "Train Ride" story about the soldier in Wyoming earlier in this book. The story that follows also came straight from a Storyteller Network Group—it is so vivid to me, it seems like a script for a film. In Mattie's words, her experience "put some scars on us that we carry forever." She adds, "It taught me not to put off loving, for anything can disappear in a moment."

The Day Our Daddy Came Home
No one wanted to shroud the young ones, the babies who died just a few days old. But I did once, a little cousin during that time after World War I when the flu from Spain struck and people everywhere got weak and feverish, and sick to their stomachs.

So many died down there in Georgia, they finally disallowed funerals altogether, burying people immediately. It was then, I remember, when the churches began filling every day, and it was at the church where we held together what we had. So we were used to the dying, my sisters and brothers and me, though I was only nine. But when it was my mama suddenly on the coolin' board, her life gone after just a few days of fever, it was not something we could understand.

And as she lay there on the wood planks that lay on top of two cane bottom chairs, some neighbor rubbed her body clean with cotton cloths, then covered her with a white sheet, put the saucer of salt on her chest, placed buffalo nickels on her eyes, and we all kept the cats out of the house. After a day or two, my daddy pulled some planks off one of the old cotton houses and made a casket that we buried her in.

In Forsythe, Georgia, in 1922, on a small farm, with six kids and no mama, life goes on. We hardly got used to doing all the new chores when one night while my daddy slept with the babies, we heard the bloodhounds barkin' and one of my daddy's friends ran into the house, and I remember everyone crying, and my oldest brother quiet and scared (knowing a little more than the rest of us). Daddy dressed real quick and told us he had to leave right away, and that would be the last we'd see of him for a long, long time.

It turned out my daddy a couple days earlier had gone down to check the corn he'd planted by the river, because there'd been heavy rains and it might have been too wet to cultivate. He came upon the Gold Dust vendor, the one-horse wagon with the canvas top, ransacked, most of the soap powder, tobacco, snuff and Cracker Jacks already gone. And the vendor, my daddy discovered, beat-up and unconscious.

Now in those days, a black man found next to an unconscious white man was a dead man. So my daddy ran fast and far way from all that. Once the word got out, the white moonshiners from across the river, who wanted my daddy's business all along, blamed him. Of course the Masonics stepped in, knowing my daddy was innocent, selling his buggy, mule and milk cow, saving him that night from a lynching and arranging for him to travel in a casket, like a dead man, on a train form Georgia to Cleveland, Ohio. I couldn't help but think of my mama in her casket, dreaming that long peaceful sleep, and my daddy in his casket, scared for his life, dreaming too of a new life, if he made it, in the North with no wife, no family, no farm.

My father's sister took me and Mary Ola, my sister. Another relative took two of my brothers and another sister. And still another relative took the baby, and we pretty much didn't see each other anymore. My sister and I were passed on to another of my father's sisters, then on to my grandmother, and all the while we could not understand how we lost our entire family so quickly that year.

We saw Daddy again ten years later, in 1932, in East Point, Georgia, where both Mary Ola and me got married. I can still see him picking up my son James, just over a year old, his grandson, into his arms and smilin' that smile we had seen so many times so many years before.

And it seemed so natural, so right. I remember, like a man stepping out of his casket, stepping out of his grief and out of his years on the run, and holding a grandson up to the light of a sky that echoed no longer with the howl of blood hounds in the night, but with the heartbeat of enduring love. 捲

(story told by Mattie Whitley; transcribed and written by Ross Talarico)

EIGHT

More Stories

EARNEST RADCLIFFE, A MAN NEARING SEVENTY, WOULDN'T TELL his story in front of the others, as we sat at our Wednesday afternoon story group just west of downtown Rochester, New York. After a while he came up to me and motioned he wanted a word with me. He was embarrassed, he told me, by the tears he knew he might shed reliving his encounters with his stepfather, his wife and her family, and his real father. "Seems like I was always leaving somewhere," said Radcliffe, "counting money in my pockets." Just seventy five cents, as a matter of fact, when he ran away from home as a young boy after protecting his brother form an ax-swinging step-pa.

When we take the time to reflect upon our lives, we focus on the touchstones of our experience, those moments which seemed to have given our lives direction, for better or for worse. In Radcliffe's story that follows, there are, surprisingly, as in a number of the stories in this book, the elements of a novel—the initiations into manhood, the sexual pursuit, the fall from grace, and the life-affirming encounter with beauty (the gladiola farm) that somehow becomes the complement to a life rising out of the ashes of dejection. As I wrote from the several pages of notes I took as Radcliffe privately told his story apart from the others, I was astonished how the pieces fell together. Of course it was the same process I am describing in this book—one detail begets another detail, one memory begets another memory—and within all these recollections, the individual, the man or woman within the storyteller, emerges and claims his or her identity. It should have hit me form the beginning; a man who feels the urge to tell a story and who feels tears welling within is the right person to tell the story!

Youth

WATERBORO, SOUTH CAROLINA

I was thirteen, maybe fourteen, the day my brother LeRoy played hooky and, though he should've known better, took our step-parents grocery money and gambled it away with those boys in the north woods. "Don't cry," I told him when he came to me, "I'll get the money back."

But they wouldn't give it back, and when we told our step-pa, it all happened so fast I don't remember the words, and when I close my eyes I see it happening again, like I'm watching an old movie that keeps getting clearer with age: My step-pa's so angry he tosses his cap and grabs onto the ax he's chopping wood with. He turns toward me, but it's LeRoy burning in his eye, and with one wild heave of that heavy oak-handled ax he moves toward my brother and starts to swing.

I picked up whatever was close, a short oak log with a couple of sharp branches sticking out. And I heaved it with all the strength and accuracy of my fear, hitting my step-pa right square on the side of his head, and he went down dropping his arms, the ax, the blood spurting from his temple like a stream. I stared at the fallen man, unconscious, just laying there, LeRoy standing over him, then looking at me. "Take care of him," I said, scared I might have killed him. "Call an ambulance," I said to LeRoy, who looked at me with such a mixture of love and fright I'll never forget. "I'm gone," I added, taking a couple of steps backward, then a few more, until I ran all the way to the bus station in town.

I had seventy-five cents in my pocket, and got off in Savannah, Georgia. I had an uncle there named *Dog*. I climbed a fence and found an open cab of a Royal Crown truck, and fell asleep. In the morning some guy woke me up, but he wasn't angry. He said I could ride deliveries with him, and later he asked, "want a job?" It made me feel good, but my belly still ached, and my mind still hurt.

DAYTONA BEACH

First the cigarette fell from Simon Fry, the regular cook's mouth, then old Simon himself, who drank more than he ought to, fell flat on his face behind the stove one day, dead drunk. And that's when I took up the fry station, turning all that meat on the steaming grill.

I was fifteen, with a lot of faith in God, and a job in the cafeteria baking cornbread, biscuits, and potato pie. Now, frying meat not only paid better, there were other benefits: I cold eat free, and more important, I could trade meat for dates with the waitresses. And that's how I met Winnie Ruth a year or so later. Before long we made our way to Nero's, a transit room where you could pay a buck and a quarter and make love for an hour. And the second time we went, I swear, she got in the family way. And before I knew it, we had four boys, a good marriage, and a bunch of in-laws that took half the money I made laying cables for Bell Telephone.

Winnie Ruth still liked making love and having babies; the more she fed me, the poorer I got. So I was probably looking for an excuse when my real father, A.L. Radcliffe, wrote me and said he was sick, and wanted to see his oldest son, and to come down to Greensville right quick. When I got there the moonshine was flowing. My daddy wasn't sick, just feeling a little to happy for his own good. I drank too, and when some dude named Jake slapped my daddy during an argument, I started a fight with him, and before I knew it I ripped a small potato knife I had from my cooking days against the flesh over his ribs. So that night, in Greensville for less than twenty-four hours, to keep peace between two families, I had to leave town, for good.

In Daytona, Winnie and her family wanted no part of me, claiming I'd fallen from sugar to you know what. I slept under the stars that night, thinking back to that Royal Crown truck in Savannah a few years earlier. It seemed like I was always hurting someone hoping to save someone else, like I was always leaving family somewhere, counting the money in my pockets.

GOING NORTH

His name was Cannonball, and I didn't believe for a minute that his old Pontiac would make it to Savannah—not Georgia, where I would have been happy to go—but Savannah, New York, up north. But what choice did I have?

So I climbed in and listened to him talk for miles on end about gladiolas—how to plant and care for them, and when we got there I pressed those seeds gently into the dirt, like I was paying my dues to the good fresh earth. And a few months later, standing in the midst of such colors under the clear blue sky, I clipped those gladiolas, their scent rising from the huge meadow of perfume, each bouquet, hundreds of them, a strange blessing to a difficult life. &

(*story told by Earnest Radcliffe; transcribed and written by Ross Talarico*)

I OFTEN REPEAT THE LAST LINE OF EARNEST RADCLIFFE'S STORY TO myself: *strange blessing to a difficult life*. That phrase seems to go to the core of what much of storytelling is all about. It is through our valiant examination of a troublesome or sorrowful moment that we discover the spirit which enables us to endure—and often to endure proudly. Love and Sadness, in the real world, go hand in hand—a writer, a storyteller, an artist, accepts this notion. The gladiolas are a beautiful symbol of what blossoms in hard times deep within human effort and will. In a sense, this story will be unlike many of the stories of others because the time-frame and breadth of the experiences are so broad. Most, the type I can recommend for you to tell in this book, will focus on single incidents, or certainly restricted time-frames. But put several of your recollections together, focusing intently on one at a time, and you will begin to construct the larger contexts, the multiple revelations that might result in an extended recollection, which is the first step toward being the author of a book!

The following story stems from something we will enjoy recollecting: A childhood memory. We tend to retell our childhood stories because we remember a particular and universal state of being: open, impressionable, and anticipatory with a strange blend of optimism and vulnerability. The next story was told to me by a judge in upstate New York, Joe Valentino. It is not, as I have noted in these explorations of storytelling throughout the book, a sensational or even an unusual story—at its heart is an initiation into a darker side of not only the world, but one's self as well. Judge Valentino tells a typical goodhearted tale about growing up with friends, playing ball, getting into minor mischief, his dog, and an old widow who strikes fear into the neighborhood kids. And yet, it is, like in so many of the stories we have experienced thus far, the thoughtfulness that gives it its sincere and meaningful core. He learns a lesson in life through contemplation of a childhood romp. It is a story, much like the other stories here, of a lesson in individual and social responsibility. And if there is a gap between the understanding of each, as there often is, that gap is synonymous with curiosity and human predicament—the true source of our stories, including those of childhood.

Queenie and the Widow
There is a hill that slopes gradually down where Brown Street meets Jefferson Avenue, and it looks much smaller today than it normally does, there, in my memory, where the Murano twins, Gregory and Laurie, blind in one eye from a scissors accident, where the twins are taking the rubber tips off their arrows during another battle between Cowboys and Indians.

We would always make it a contest between the forces of good and evil, soldiers, cops and robbers, always a war of sorts, one man ready to eliminate another. But it was always fun, good hearted, as if somehow we simply separated the good and the bad, and of course we knew we were good and honest and committed to the welfare of everyone around us—an enemy one day was your sidekick the next, charging up and down the hill on Brown Street.

So the day Tonto came to town, I mean TONTO—Jay Silverheels himself, the *Lone Ranger's* sidekick, and stayed, actually sleeping and eating over a couple of streets in our neighborhood at his brother-in-law's house, our world changed a bit. I met him, shook his hand, and somehow he brought our neighborhood into the blue light of Televised America, where I could lay back with my head resting on Queenie, our family's Collie, and know that whatever was on the radiating tube was just a few steps down a road we could all take someday, if we followed our dreams past Main Street, past Chili Avenue, past Buffalo Road and out West under skies so blue and clear.

Queenie, though, seemed very content in our neighborhood, following me everywhere, to school if someone forgot to tie her, to Deramo's Grocery Store (now Padilla's), and to the empty lot where she'd chase butterflies while we chased fly balls, or chase us on the bases, or lay down in centerfield. Everyone liked her, except Aunt Kutuzza, who lived upstairs from us and complained bitterly when Queenie barked and ate her flowers. As a matter of fact, it is Queenie I think of today, here, in my middle-age years, remembering, as men seem to, companionship during the early years. There was something in our neighborhood between the dogs and kids, something that defined the trust we'd seek in others as the years passed. Queenie was always there, running next to me as I rode my bike in the afternoons, there on the steps of the porch when everyone gathered in the twilight dialogue of our wondrous "idle hours." So I reflect with a nagging sense of guilt when I remind myself that I was the cause of Queenie being sent away...

It was instinct, I swear, when it came to gathering together; we'd just walk out the door—Gregory, Laurie, Jay, Mike, Pat and myself—and we'd know where to go, the corner hill, the grocery store, of the empty lot next to "The Neighborhood Widow." She haunted us, always dressed in black, the black shawl, black stockings, black shoes, no matter what the season, the temperature, or the current fashions. Here house was next to the field where we played baseball and football, and every once in a while a ball would go over, and she'd be there, as if she were waiting just that moment, and that dark, solitary figure would appear, her scowl leaving us speechless, her Italian not poetry, but a language guttural, threatening, and as dark as the shadow she cast. She'd pick up the ball, stare at us, and make her way back to her house, and many times that was the end of our ball game.

We never did know her name, just *The Neighborhood Widow*, and to us she represented an adult world that had no sensitivity to children, and because she never spoke a word of English, she represented too the dark side of Italian; the brooding, sinister interior we all secretly suspect is a part of our own being, so it

scares us even more. One day Jay's football flew over the fence
into her yard. It was too early in the afternoon to do nothing, so,
in a fit of rebellious courage, I jumped the wooden fence and
crouched down making my way through the uncut bushes and
weeds. My friend's silence seemed to echo behind me. My
heart was pounding when I saw the football under a brush. I
leaped forward, grabbed the ball, and in a moment of victory I
stood up holding the ball and waving it over my head.

It happened very quickly, a shadow over me, a broom whisk-
ing through the air, that strange language filling me with terror,
and suddenly the chase was on. As I ran toward the fence, feeling sure I would be snatched and enfolded in a swarm of black
clothing, a blur of golden brown fur ran past me. As I jumped
the fence I saw the widow running back to her house and
Queenie hitting her at full stride, and then, to my disbelief, my
dog biting her posterior and ripping her black dress as she lay in
the jungle of her yard. Queenie, mouth open, eyes sparkling,
looked content that evening, lying on her blanket by her bowl,
but there was a "conference" going on in my aunt's kitchen, and
I was sent up to my room. I feared the worst, and later that
evening, when my parents told me that Queenie would have to
go, I felt for the first time a sense of injustice, that something
terribly wrong was being done, though I understood, in some
adult way, that decisions had to be made with the consideration
of all those around you. I guess that was part of growing up.

The next day, when I came home, the house was too quiet,
her blanket gone, her dish gone. And going out on the porch,
where Queenie was happiest, where she'd wag her tail and look
at me with sparkling eyes, I knew she was gone for good. But I
still see Queenie at times, making her way through the weeds
and bushes of the Neighborhood Widow's yard, and sometimes
I see the old woman moving her black shawl and calling in elo-

quent English, Queenie, Queenie… And I catch a glimpse of a beautiful smile and golden hair, and she and the dog walk off together toward the hill at Brown Street, where everything, for a brief while, is reconciled and okay. ✍

(story told by Joe Valentino; transcribed and written by Ross Talarico)

THE LAST IMAGE IN JOE VALENTINO'S STORY IS ONE OF CONCILIATION as he imagines somehow the incident resolving itself through wishful thinking. We often tell a story, in fact, to clarify a conflict which has gone unresolved through the years. In the case of this story, the dog redeems himself by becoming non-aggressive and the widow shows a side of herself that was never apparent in Joe Valentino's childhood experiences. We always seek other alternatives, other renderings to ease our guilt, other endings to affirm our sense of togetherness. Like the narrator says in his story, early on in the story in fact, in describing his childhood games with his friends, " we would always make it a contest between the forces of good and evil… " Good stories, the kind that reveal human character, explore not just the differences between good and evil but the connection between those two forces, the duality of their existence within an individual. That's why certain stories have a haunting and compelling nature. In them is an essential identity crisis we want to resolve, sometimes enthusiastically, sometimes reluctantly.

Here is another childhood story, but this one is not typical or delightful in anyway. It is a story from a time in our past as American immigrants when certain experiences were kept secret, hushed-up in fact because, unlike today, to speak of abusive behavior within a family was taboo. I like the following story, a story told by Helen Johnson, because the metaphor is so powerful and fitting for America: the outside of the "mansion" is beautiful and impressive, but inside it is not only empty, but a place where abuse resides. It is an image essential to the kind of identity we embrace as a part of the American Dream—the grand illusion of the prospering family.

The Mansion

My father was a carpenter and I can see him standing in the streaks of light touching the gumwood trim in the newly finished sun parlor. I can see my mother holding her hands over the small fire burning like a stray thought in the massive brick fireplace. I see myself leaning against the leaded glass of the doors that lead to the library, the shelves empty of course, and my vision a rainbow of confusion.

There was no furniture except some old crates and mattresses. I made up stories to keep my friends out as they walked home from school and stopped to admire the stately mansion they called my home. But it was temporary. Soon the house was sold, and we moved on, my father packing his tools. For a few months we lived well, enough coal to heat the half built rooms, chicken, dried carrots, cabbage and pierogi. But before long, as the house took shape, and the walls were plastered, and the fireplaces bricked, and the doors fitted with bronze hardware, it was back to noodles and rice.

And that would have been all right, except for the beatings and the cold stare of my father who seemed to love his work but not his life. I remember locking a bathroom door with my mother inside and hiding the key, and my father pounding on the door as he had often pounded on her. But he would not destroy such a rich finished oak door.

One day he dragged a steamer trunk in to the barren vestibule and onto the front porch. *Badz zdrowa*, he said without any emotion at all; it means, in Polish, stay well. And when a small pickup truck pulled up, and he got in, that's the last we saw of him. We looked at each other, at the sparseness of the huge room, of our lives to that point, and we held onto each other until the fire went out. ℘

(story told by Helen Johnson; transcribed and written by Ross Talarico)

WHEN YOU BEGIN YOUR STORYTELLER NETWORK GROUP, OR EVEN if you begin working on your story simply by yourself, it is a good idea to explore an "untold story," or a story with a few important parts of it which remain untold, or obscure, or not revealed for one reason or another. I can't tell you how many individuals harbor these untold stories. From a psychological or cultural viewpoint, one can understand why these stories exist. But artistically, these kinds of stories are essential to the story-teller as well—since their very existence suggest the compulsion that gives a story its sense of urgency and meaning, not to mention the sense of discovery which lies at the heart of any effec-tive narrative. Behind the mansion, Helen Johnson tells us—because she feels the need to tell us however painful the experience of telling it—behind the fantasy existence, the rich and decorative surface of our lives, lies the heart-aching center of an individual's true existence. The fire burns in the fireplace of the empty house to remind us of how these two people, mother and daughter, held onto each other in order to survive, and that too is part of the story, though to get there we have to go through a painful journey.

The next story of an "ordinary" person's account of his early family history takes us into interiors of other places and times, the way good stories often do. Americans are either fortunate or cursed to have an abundance of these stories since so much of our identity comes from our ancestral journey to the New World. Of course our experiences and our family's experience fill in the great void of textbooks which celebrate the immigration to America and the building of a great country. Nothing, as we know, comes easy. Sometimes someone in a storytelling group can be asked a simple question—*how did you get here*, or *how did your family get here?* It is a question whose answer can fill volumes. It is, of course, nothing less then our history, and what we have forgotten in our media-saturated, cliché-ridden overviews which sadly have become education dogma for too many of us, is that history is nothing less than an accumulation and critical rendering of personal histories. Each one of us, it is my belief, has a responsibility to record, sometime or another in our lives, a personal, articulated footnote to the larger perspective. *We are history.*

The next story, by Lucky Nahum, a businessman in upstate New York, an Italian-Jew who never considered himself a writer or a storyteller, is, in my opinion, an important contribution to our understanding not only of the logistics of history and a personal memoir, but an insightful rendering of the psychological and emotional make-up of those who came to America to essentially survive.

Learning to Whisper
We leaned into the curve keeping our balance, there, along the pink sand and blue waters of Bermuda, the moped beneath us, our love surrounding us, lifting us, as we made our way to a new life together.

It was our honeymoon; Maria looked so beautiful as I turned to glimpse her profile, her hair blowing in the warm wind. I was just twenty-one, but I knew my life had changed forever, forever, once more. At the turn toward Horseshoe Bay there was a smell in the air, a perfume that seeped through me, a fragrance that had touched my memory. I stopped and we got off the moped, and by the side of the road my new wife pointed to a field of purple flowers, a beautiful lavender contour that filled the air with its perfume. It was the Passion Flower, its fluid, purple, perfect stamen reaching out like a sea urchin, its pungent odor taking me back, back in time… ten years back to a moment when the perfumed air seemed strange and unaccounted for there in the streets of Tripoli, there where fear held us at its immobilizing attention; there, where we hid for days at a time, and where the passion flower bloomed as a symbol of hope, and where we learned how to whisper amidst ourselves in order to survive.

June 6, 1967. A friend stops by our house, whispers to our parents, and the world changes. It was the beginning of the Israeli-Arab war, and community of Italian-Jews in Tripoli had prepared themselves for the possibility. That day we made our way to a farm a few miles from the city. The Moroccan army could already be seen marching in the streets. We had already passed some Jews that had been taken away and killed by soldiers. At the farm we had food and shelter, but my parents looked worried, and my brother and I discovered it was not only because we had to hide from the Arabs, but because our presence at the farm endangered others there as well.

So under the twilight cover, just before curfew, we made our way back to our house in the city. We had to switch cars, and simply pray we wouldn't be stopped. When we discovered we had left the house keys back at the farm with our car, my mother made a daring drive past curfew, past the soldiers to the farm and back, while my father and I hid in the garage with a spear gun form our scuba equipment to protect us. Once in the house, we had to hide for days, a whole month really, fearing someone would break in and take us away forever.

I remember whispering to my brother Armando, and my mother whispering, and my father learning to whisper, and I'm afraid, like many at that time, he learned too well. We wrote notes and read to pass the hours. Neighbors secretly passed food and cigarettes and alcohol over the back wall, and that's how we survived. We had a good life in Libya; my father was a tailor, and sold liquor to oil companies. Tripoli was experiencing the last few years of colonialism, and the people there were happy, as I was, with friends in our school uniforms dancing through the streets of Tripoli, our parents with their dinner parties, inviting friends from everywhere, including the American businessmen from the army where my father had a lot of liquor business. I remember mom putting the final stitches on a dress she modeled for her sons before going off to one of the dances at the NCO or the Mocambo Club. The Italian-Jews were free-spirited, open, content with their culture and the companionship of others.

All that ended on June 6, 1967. Moroccan troops could be heard constantly in the streets from the bedroom where we hid in the darkness, and whispered our thoughts, the way men do it seems when praying for something so good it humbles us to speak of our needs. We whispered for a drink of water, for something to eat, a piece of fruit or a slice of bread. We whispered encouragement to each other, and rhymes from our childhood; and once in a while, a dream that would appear on the screen of silence where we directed our eyes for hours at a time.

One afternoon, two Arab businessmen came to our house, slipped inside and had a meeting with my father. That day a Volkswagon van pulled up to our front door so close there wasn't room for sunlight between the house and the car. We crept in quietly with the four suitcases we were allowed. In them, my mother stashed mostly photos, and clothes—and one suitcase held engineering books for my brother Armando. My father was given five choices from HIAS: Israel, Italy, Australia, Canada, or the United States. Although my parents thought of going to Israel, because they had cousins there, they choose America, because my father knew businessmen from the Army base and he thought there was a future there. From the van we got into a bus, and during the night we drove with others to the airport, getting not one, but two flat tires on the way. I remember the fear on everyone's faces as we waited for the tires to be changed, not knowing if we would be ambushed and shot there in the woods on the side of the road. At the airport we were strip-searched, and allowed, besides our four suitcases, 25 sterling lbs. to take with us. I remember it all happening so fast that I closed my eyes trying to keep somehow that image of our good life in Tripoli. And sometimes I feel my eyes are still closed trying to recapture it...

We were sent to Rochester, a tailoring town, for my father to find work. A couple met us at the airport, Isaac and Ines, who were our only friends for the longest time. They opened their house to us on Lowell Street, and my father found a job as a tailor at Bonds. After several months, we found an apartment to rent on Conkey Avenue, and my father was relieved not to take any more money from HIAS. Angela, my mother, also worked at Bonds, piecework. One day she noticed a woman with a strange twitch in the lunchroom. She was about to suggest a remedy when she realized that the movement mirrored the mechanics of her body as she worked at her machine. Life would be different in America.

Armando went to beautician school, the architect books put away in a closet, still heavy but useless. On Conkey Avenue everyone was busy except me, and it was not a happy time. I was fed, given a home, but the warmth was gone: we had all grown up too quickly, no more hugs, simply sitting together, mama and papa too busy working, too tired at night. The cold weather was equally repressive. Armando was old enough to be with his own friends. My parents were still attached to the old culture of Tripoli, creating a kind of sadness I hadn't seen before. No more dancing at the NCO club at the American base, or at the Mocambo club. Mom and dad seemed to leave so much of themselves behind.

I felt suddenly as if I had no one, no identity, not Jewish, not Italian. I made my way to School 8, not knowing anyone, being laughed at, I remember, for putting my raincoat and boots in the hallway, thinking America was too poor to put hooks on the walls. I made my way to the back of the room, with other immigrants, sitting in-between two Puerto Rican boys. Yes, we were lucky, like my name, to survive 1967, but in America we all led separate lives.

Emotionally, we had to fend for ourselves.

(story told by Lucky Nahum; transcribed and written by Ross Talarico)

I'LL ALWAYS REMEMBER WHEN LUCKY NAHUM SPOKE THE LINE, *emotionally, we had to fend for ourselves.* I believe these words, these articulates insights into life's experience, comes as a result of reliving a part of our lives through the clarity of which only a story makes us aware. Lucky's story is a recollection of displacement—both literally and metaphorically. So many of us feel displaced, and in a culture void of meaningful human contact on a daily basis, in a culture of alienation, being displaced leads to resentment, anger, hostility, fear and aggression. The secret is to get through the negative responses and discover what's at the heart of human existence, discover the affirmation of life as do singers, artists, musicians, writers. Let me state it as simply as possible: to tell one's story, to tell it honestly and feel compelled to recreate what seems significant and meaningful as you do, is to unveil the hope and love that drives the species to a wondrous fulfillment. These stories aren't about winning the lottery. This last one is about war itself. I don't think I'm being overly optimistic by saying that the telling of a story represents a challenge to perception and a query into character. Something emerges as a story unfolds—some notion, some deeply human assessment, or some person who has been guided by—remember those words—*wisdom and a sense of community, often in the midst of confusion and isolation.*

The next story is a short tale about America. It involves a brief recollection of a time when urban riots began touching our neighborhoods and our sense of separation, prejudice, and eventually our overcoming of barriers between races, classes, and individuals in our country. Rose Muscarella creates a portrait of a neighborhood scene involving Italian-Americans, state police, and blacks during a time when people were too confused to see or heal themselves. What she remembers, and what she so vividly and succinctly recalls, is her black neighbor singing and playing the piano in the midst of all that violence and hatred—a time I can remember because I was growing up in that neighborhood where white neighborhoods brought shot guns to their porches the way Rose's husband does in her story. It echoes what we just discussed in the previous story about the journey from Tripoli to America—overcoming the alienation, the anger and aggression to find that artistic moment, that affirmation of life, somewhere in the midst of those moments. "Tillie's" song at the piano is the symbol of that humanity-nurturing experience that somehow emerges. Am I saying that one important aspect of storytelling is an assessment of our own prejudices and discriminatory tendencies, that storytelling actually is therapeutic in breaking down barriers between races and classes in America? Yes, I am.

The State Troopers

They sat down in the lawn chairs we set up for them in our backyard. There was a love seat swing with wrought iron arms and Italian flowers pressed into the metal seat. They seemed to enjoy it.

Once in while when we heard a gunshot echo through the neighborhood, one of the troopers would shake his head, put on his hat, and walk down the driveway and look up and down the street. Later, we moved the coffee pot to the front porch. Some of the neighbors would stop over; perhaps because of the troopers being there.

But my husband Joe got out his shotgun anyway, and stood on the front steps, like a soldier from another time, another place. One of the troopers, with his hand on Joe's shoulder, talked him into putting the gun back in the attic. I made some lemonade against the intermittent sirens of the streets.

Even the black family next door came over to stay with us. They seemed more afraid than we were. Tillie was an entertainer, playing the piano for the rich in another part of the city. She played for us one night; the troopers gathered around the piano, clapping their hands and singing with their huge voices. We all laughed so hard we forgot about the looting and the shooting, and the bad feelings and calloused hands gripping rocks and sticks during the racial riots of 1964. ᴂ

(*story told by Rose Muscarella; transcribed and written by Ross Talarico*)

BEFORE I MOVE ON TO THE NEXT STORY IN THIS CHAPTER, I WANT to point out, using the "State Troopers" story, just how important context is in your storytelling attempts. If we placed the piano incident in a different context—at birthday party or at the end of an evening of drinking and conversation with friends for example—it would convey an entirely different meaning. Let the story be a reminder to us that the **background**, whether it be geographical, sociological, or psychological, is an essential part of your storytelling success. We have to see and feel the background against which the focused moment takes place. It is part of the larger perspective within which the individual experience takes on both self-identity and uniqueness.

Rose Muscarella's story, though short and understated, captures for me the essence of human relationship even amidst
the fear, anger and violence that torments our society.

FINALLY, I INCLUDE A NARRATIVE FROM AN ORAL HISTORY BY AN
eighty year-old Native American woman who told me her story
after I asked her about a photo on her desk, a photo of four
women: herself as a child, her mother, her grandmother, and
her great grandmother. She then began to tell me her story,
which went back almost a hundred and fifty years, the story of
early bonds with white men, of Indians being forced from their
native lands, but also the story of individuals and their struggles
to survive, and emerge with their dignity and pride.

Native American, Truly American
There is a photograph on a wall in the Cultural Center at Pala,
and in it I see myself being held by a woman whose warmth I
can feel now, as always, even in my own chilly afternoon of
these 80 life years…

She is my great grandmother, Manuella Griffith, singing me
songs, coyote or owl, always a little lilt to let me know what was
coming next. *Sibimoat* was her Indian name, from the *Cupeno*
tribe, meaning "the people who slept here"—which described
their mellow temperament, how they never changed anything,
simply people of the valley. She was born around 1850, and met
her husband, a white cattleman from Oklahoma, about twenty-
five years later, a man named Fred who drove cattle and horses
across the prairies and mountains.

He was a handsome man, and I'm not sure what he saw in
her, except that the sparkle I saw in her eyes as a child, that
warm, wise, loving spark that made her smile so reassuring, that
sparkle must have been perceived by adults as well, that invitation into our own humanity. I see it, feel it, in the photo even

now, her dark face, her caring hands around me. She was a tiny thing, very dark but very warm and soft, with a gift for giving comfort to others. She was used to her husband leaving for long periods of time, and I imagine she'd see him there in the dark horizons of the distant mountains in the early evenings of her simple desires in Warner Springs.

It was during one of his long cattle-drives through Texas when she found out he had taken sick, and sometime after that she learned he had died. It turned out that he had left her some cattle, otherwise the only thing she received was a photo of him sent by his father in Boston, and a necklace of blue Venetian beads that one could only get form the east coast. She wore them always—I never remember her without them around her neck, a romantic tie to her husband.

I was about seven when she died. She'd come to Pala with the others in the Removal of 1903 (when her tribe was forced out of its home under government supervision). At first they lived in tents, then in portable houses, the kits that came from New York that were government-issued. They were strong little homes, basically two rooms, a bedroom and a kitchen. Pala was a beautiful village at that time. All the yards had bushes and flowers and gardens. Every year prizes were given for the most beautiful yards. There was, at once, a sense of community and a sense of pride. The lots, as small as they were, belonged to people. Pala was laid out like a city, allotments structured to parallel the main road and revolve around the mission, the lovely Mission San Antonio de Pala, where our spirits met and spread forth like the soft echoes of laughter and prayers. Irrigation was put in, a store built, Salmon's, which had a post office, and where Indians could go and charge their groceries. Of course The Removal had broken us somewhat, changed our people.

But we created a sense of community in Pala, even though we may have sensed things would change again.

Salvadora, my grandmother, daughter of Manuela, owned property on the other side of the river. She was tall, just the opposite of her mother. She was diffcrent too, realizing that unlike the women of her mother's generation, she had to be a provider, not just for my mother and my Aunt Catherine, her two daughters whom she brought to Pala in the Removal of 1903, but to so many others as a teacher in the schools, an organizer in the Pala community where she directed others to learn trades, like carpentry for the men, and domestic science (housekeeping) at schools like Sherman so the women could make good livings taking care of homes in Los Angcles and even Beverly Hills—where Salvadora herself, to make money to build her house in Pala, worked as a governess for a while. She was a businesswoman too, renting out land to Mr. Moreno who grew chiles, green Ortega chiles that the Native American women would hang and dry in the fields, and as a result Mr. Moreno, a good man, would gencrously share his profits with the Indians. She taught others how to weave and sew, and even initiated accounts with Mr. Fulton, I believe that was his name, a friend of Mr. Robinson of Robinson's department stores, for whom she had been a governess, to produce altar cloths and bobbin lace from fine linen for the Pala mission. She also taught the young people Catechism and lessons for First Communion. She canned more apricots and peaches than anyone, her house filled with glass jars and the boiled lids that would seal the fruit, and she'd give much of it away, always giving to others who didn't have as much. In a way, she wasn't very demonstrative, but she was a matriarch for the whole village, teaching the kids who were coming from the mountains to bathe and brush their teeth, and making sure the girls had dresses for church. She was a disciplinarian with imagination and a good heart. Salvadora was loved by many, but she was a hero to me.

In 1909 she built the new house, which still stands in Pala today. It was big and beautiful, with four bedrooms, three of which Salvadora planned to rent out for a dollar a night. At that time prospectors were coming from all over, New York, Germany, England… to Temecula and Pala and Julian to see about buying land for ranches and farms, cattle and fruit trees—even apple trees in Julian. But there were also professors and historians coming to Pala, to study the ways of the Indians here, their customs, their myths, their songs and dances, their appreciation of the earth itself. So the rooms were rented much of the time. I still have the register, and it's easy for me to dream of the nights on the porch when I would overhear the strangers speaking about so many things, bringing their worlds to the quiet Pala air of our early evenings, drinking tea and Salvadora's fry-bread (now they call them Indian tacos). I remember learning about the constellations from Marie Walsh, a historian, who recorded many of our stories and stayed many times at our house, and every time I look at the sky at night, I remember those days. So it was our lives we were sharing, there in the peace of our small village, the tribal songs and stories of Manuela and Salvadora jotted down by strangers who wanted to know more about us, just as my story here is written on the page of our universal souls. I would fill the basins and pitchers in the rooms, and serve coffee. I felt often I was in a soap opera, and I had, and will always have, a sense of oneness, all these things going on in our small place in the world. There was no one else living in the house but me and my grandmother. And she was the center of it all—not that she had an easy life. She too married a cowboy, a Spanish/Indian man called Valenzuela from the

Mesa Grande. She had two children with him, my mother, Claudina, and my Aunt Catherine. But she divorced him, with papers in fact, and my one great disappointment for her was that she never remarried. Maybe she was too giving of others. Maybe her strength required a certain personal loneliness. She too received cattle from Manuela, and then she sent her two girls (my mother and my aunt) to Banning to get a good education at the Catholic schools. And she went to work as a governess to L.A. and Beverly Hills where she took care of a young boy from a wealthy family who spent a lot of time in Europe. And that's where, by the way, she formed her extravagant habit of buying and wearing a variety of lovely and sometimes audacious hats from the many hat stores in Los Angeles. It became the trademark of her appearance in Pala, and it became the trademark of my mother's as well. And of course as close as I was to Salvadora, who was more of a mother to me than anyone, I cannot tell the story of four generations of Native American women without telling you about my mother.

It's not that she didn't love me any less than a mother should, nor I her, but there were circumstances, and that's why I spent most of my growing years living with Salvadora, my grandmother. I will say this, my mother too took on the tradition of owning and wearing a variety of incredible hats—but she wasn't blessed with Salvadora's fortitude, or her health. My mother had tuberculosis. There were times we couldn't get close to her, times when she was coughing and had headaches, but never complained. I remember how my relatives would go up to her room and put slices of Irish potatoes around her head in a cloth. After a while, the potatoes would turn black, an Indian remedy, supposedly drawing out the poison from her head.

As a matter of fact it was her sickness that kept me from my father, a Swiss named Charles Heckman, a baker of fine pastries my mother met in L.A. where she worked as a domestic caretaker in Beverly Hills. She married him and I was born in L.A., but I came back to Pala when I was four to live with Salvadora. By that time my father was moving up to Solvang to work with the Dutch and Swiss population up there, and the marriage was more or less over. And my mother, afraid she would die early, wanted me to be with her family in Pala and not her husband's European relatives. So I saw little of him. I would be fifteen when he died. I'd go back and forth between Pala and Los Angeles when I was little, on the train by myself often, all dressed up in the pretty L.A. dresses my mother would buy me (I tried wearing them in Pala, but my friends didn't like them, thought I was being arrogant and superficial, so I kept them in a chest). I remember wearing a big tag on my chest, with my name and destination, and the red caps, black men with bow-ties, taking great care of me as they helped me with my doll and my suitcase. I liked both places, really, but I saw more of Pala and less of L.A., and I felt a kind of yearning that Manuela and Salvadora felt for the land, a natural reverence the *Cupenos* felt as people of the valley. My mother struggled, with her sickness, with her life. She embodied the separation that marked our people as far back as 1903 and The Removal, when my ancestors, including Manuela and Salvador, were told to walk off from their home, that it wasn't theirs anymore. It is some journey, and it is a journey inward as well. No, I never felt any lack of love whatsoever from my mother, and I loved her as well. It's just that over the years it was Salvadora who was there for me and for so many in Pala, and her strength kept us together, filled us with love, the acceptance of hard work, and the patience and good will that truly marked the Native American population, whatever was left of it.

I returned in 1963. And I'm here for good, eighty years of letting the spirit of the good earth here pass through me like a song. The house Salvadora built still stands, a sturdy reminder of her perseverance. I still feel the warmth of Manuela, that inner glow that gives true light to the eyes that see through time. And my mother's love shines too through her frail body as she waves from the train station in L.A. I was a lucky little girl. Oh, sometimes I'd resent having to bring in the wood at Salvadora's house, wondering why so many men disappeared from our lives. But I remember too how Salvadora would make the fire warm and bright in our room so I could study at night. The truth is we embodied all the strange aspects of the dominant-culture-the difficult days of the cattle-drives, the ways of prospectors and European speculators, the Spanish influence of the mission in the midst of poverty, the journeys to Catholic schools and the domestic science training academics for the Indian women, the split-up families, the journeys back to Pala... and the will to be ourselves. 🠒

(story told by Nadeen Nelson; transcribed and written by Ross Talarico)

NINE

Summary:
Subversion, Companionship
and a Tribute to Friends

I CAN'T HELP BUT RETURN TO THE INEVITABLE CONCERN FOR OUR
children as I try to summarize the need for storytelling to flourish once again in our society. The violent and disastrous event at
Columbine High School in Colorado and at other schools
throughout the country, were met with all kinds of speculation
on both the causes and resolutions for the sudden epidemic of
violent encounters directed toward companions by disturbed
and alienated people. The discussions covered particular agenda items from gun control to the effects of violent video games
to the lack of parental supervision and so forth. It's not that any
of these issues lack legitimacy, but if we look at the larger context surrounding what seems to be lacking in our young people's
experience, we might perceive an inability to put things into
context, or in a meaningful perspective. The two words at the
center of this book—*wisdom and community*—are also the fundamental words which are the basic building blocks of a true
sense of context. Our children, like ourselves, actually, but more
ingrained in their ensuing sense of self, have a random, confused, and disconnected understanding of how events in their
own lives as well as events in the world around them fit together.

We haven't mentioned the place of *organization*. Storytelling
is all about organization. Being a writer and a lecturer, I can't

tell you how many people have approached me with the line, I've got a story to tell, or who have the conviction that, placing hand on chest, they have a novel right inside them. I try to be suggestive instead of skeptical hoping those who approach me will be encouraged to focus on particulars, to sort out one experience from another, and find a way to be comfortable trying to come to terms with difficult memories. I hope they will make the time to go through that strange ritual of articulation, which clarifies vague but powerful emotions and unites them with a detailed account of an event. That is the unification that leads to human awareness, and helps us understand eventually under what circumstances human beings react the way they do.

Of course this is what the book is all about, taking the time to recollect and sort out experiences for a reason: to discover the best in ourselves, or at least our own potential for discovering and rediscovering the vitality of our humanity. I find it odd in writing that last sentence, I realize that in trying to get to the basics of human expression I have resorted to our classic understanding of drama and narrative, and their purposes, from our Greek teachers, the playwrights and priests who invited people to take a quick glimpse into their souls in order to see their humanistic potential. Perhaps there is a shorter line than we imagine between basic and classic. Storytelling just hasn't changed in its purpose and value to a culture. And it isn't that we feel less compelled to communicate our experiences to each other as individuals. What, then, has changed?

Speed and Convenience are two categories listed in the student-friendly questionnaire at a very profitable "adult" university in Southern California. In fact, many institutions promote such concepts in trying to attract students in what has become a very profitable business in America, higher education; the selling point is simple, the "new student" in our country encountering courses and programs that are not as time-consuming and rigorous as traditional educational programs in the past, and with new technologies available, there is plenty of "information" on hand to satisfy anyone's surface needs—once again, *information as opposed to knowledge and perspective*. This, to me, is symptomatic of the times we live in. There is too much to do and not enough time to do it. So we embrace the "information age," where we are, on top of the stress and hectic pace of our existing lives, bombarded suddenly with the availability of so much information we suddenly feel immobilized, even more dependent on sound bites, instant analysis, cliché responses, bullet memos, paraphrases, overviews, stereotypes, and a fear of our own natural desires to go deeper into the realm of human understanding. Storytelling, in effect, in our society fraught with "story-substitutes," has become no less than a subversive activity. If this were a totalitarian state, considering the consumer-based culture in which we live, storytelling would be banned.

So it comes to this. I'm asking you in this book to become subversive, to challenge the status quo, to turn your back for a while on speed and convenience, and to try to put a hold on all that information that you can flip through and disregard with the ease of a finger on a computer board or a channel switcher. Going back to the subject of our confused, disconnected children at the beginning of this chapter, they need some quiet, reflective, wise activity from their elders, something to ease their fears and make them believe again in the potential of our human capacity for companionship. Tell your story. Tell your little stories. In this day and age, considering our frantic existence, you will be a part of a social revolution. Here's a brief checklist if you're ready:

- Turn off the T.V.
- Reread this book.
- Concentrate on just one or two recollections.
- Write a few details on a pad.
- Be open to other thoughts.
- Try to organize the details.
- Capture the context of your story.
- Talk to someone else about it.
- Meet with others in a group.
- Probe for details within yourselves.
- Complete one story before going on to others.
- Share that story, spoken or read, with others—family, strangers, especially children.

You didn't know, did you, how easily you could become a radical—someone who challenges the status-quo. You didn't believe it could be so enjoyable. You didn't realize you would be in such good company—Thoreau, Whitman, Lincoln, Twain, Kuralt, Keillor.

And, finally, what you will recognize in others as you join a Story Group, and in yourself even if it is a private encounter with your muse, what you will see emerging from the page, in the faces of others, in the mirror when you take a good look at yourself as a storyteller does, what you will see is that what matters more than anything in our attempts to identify ourselves at any given time is not simply fortune or circumstance, but character (*each face becomes its true face*).

I CONCLUDE NOW THE WAY I BEGAN THIS BOOK, WITH MY OWN compulsion to tell a story about my father, who died when I was eighteen. I hope in my simple desires to tell some stories here that I've helped others to begin telling their own. Remember, you may think your story is very private, its meaning and significance known only to yourself. That may be true, but there are thousands of people out there who would love to hear it.

My Father

My mom and I got home about the same time, almost five in the afternoon, she from her work at the shoe factory, me from the community college where I was taking classes. I wanted, in fact, to go away to school, leap forward into another kind of life, to become a writer and be both adventuresome and reflective about my young life growing up among great friends and family in upstate New York. But we didn't expect all this, my father contracting some mysterious staphylococcus germ after an operation to replace parts of his aorta, and being sick and in and out of the hospital for a year and a half.

We warmed up soup, had some toast with it, and then we got in the car to make our nightly trip to Strong Memorial Hospital, where my father lay half-dazed from the drugs, getting worse, the staphylococcus filling him with infection—the only thing keeping him alive was his heart, the big strong kind, a heart conditioned no doubt by the love he gave and received.

We met my sister Lonnie there, and when she saw us in the hallway, her eyes were red and she had this strange, sad little smile on her face. "I just came out from him," she said, nodding toward his room, "he's humming away, seems as happy as can be." Then she broke down again, and we all hugged each other. My father was humming because the staphylococcus had traveled up to his brain and he had been hallucinating. He didn't even realize, in fact, that the doctors had cut off his leg, right up to the knee, because the germ had strangled blood vessels and decayed the flesh. Every night for two weeks the doctors had prepared us for the worst, most nights telling us he probably wouldn't last the night. But like I said, he had this big strong heart, and years later, as a writer, I would understand how natural and appropriate metaphors can be.

Sure enough, when I entered the room with my mom and went to the side of the bed and held my dad's hand, he began singing the song made famous by The Ink Spots—*I'm gonna sit right down and write myself a letter, and make-believe it came from you...* I sang it with him as he lay there, delirious, eyes closed, but with a satisfied smile on his face. He was such a wonderful human being. I sang with him, the tears in my eyes, my own untested heart breaking. And it was then I remember when my own particular notion of heaven and hell came to me. Since my father and my family always sat around the kitchen table talking about ideas, the question of an afterlife always came up. I'm not sure if we described ourselves as agnostics or what, but the conversations at our table were always exciting and probing, and I imagine my love of literature and poetry started there with my father's curiosity and love as my mother poured coffee for all of us at the table. I thought to myself, I remember, as I saw him slipping away and knowing somehow I would not see him again ever except in my dreams, that perhaps the test of the nature of one's soul came at death. I simplified it: if you seem happy and content, well, that's what heaven is all about. If you're miserable, maybe there's a reason.

Later, we sung Frankie Lane's song—*just direct your feet to the sunny side of the street*. And, like always, my sister and mother and I gave my dad a long, loving look before we left for the night. Like I said, I was taking classes at the local community college, and because of my father's condition, his sickness at home and in the hospital, I missed a few classes that semester. But I kept up with my work and papers due and tests and so forth. I didn't expect any privileged treatment, although I hoped my professors might be sympathetic to what I was going through. I do remember one history teacher, an Italian, Fabiano I believe, saying with empathy it would be okay to skip one test.

About three weeks after my father died, my speech professor handed out a list of punitive assignments for those who missed classes. I had missed several, but I had done all my speeches at the correct times and managed pretty well at that. I looked at the list and there at the very bottom was my name: *9 missed classes, 9 papers due*. I threw up my hand feeling sure some mistake had been made. At nineteen one still believed in justice. I said that my absences had been excused, that they couldn't be helped, and that I had done all my work for the class.

She cut me off in mid-sentence, looked at me with such a vicious smile I shivered in the warm, stuffy air of the old brick building. "What was your excuse anyhow, Mr. Talarico?" She spoke with such condemnation that when I opened my mouth nothing came out. I had told her, as I had my other teachers, about the situation involving my father. If I would have said my father died I would have burst out in tears in front of the whole class. I put one hand over my eyes and uttered something like *never mind please*.

A couple days later my friends showed up, one by one, each with one of the nine papers I had due during the week I was catching up and studying for finals. Oh, I knew about plagiarism and its illicit and illegal nature. Later in life as a professor I would see colleagues in the English department getting so excited about plagiarism that, between the choking and spasms of their obsessions, they wrote up regulations stating that every idea a student obtained from another source, whether it be from a parent, roommate, or a television commercial, had to be notated at the bottom of a page. It struck me that such a practice might alter my writing style, a small text, a couple of sentences or so, and a Joycean page of footnotes. Personally, I had always equated original thought with original sin: it wasn't a matter of how many existed (I'd say not too many), it was how many unique ways you found to express them that counted in the long run.

My friends had been terrific all during my dad's stay at the hospital and at his death, bringing me notes from classes so I wouldn't fall behind. This time they had organized their efforts, each friend doing a paper. It was a great learning experience for me. Not the papers, they were just punishment. It was, of course, the kind of experience at the core of our efforts to know more about ourselves and our associates and our relationships with each other; in other words, our humanity. For me, it put things into perspective: education had to do with developing our human resources. My friends' generosity came from a wisdom much deeper and more communal than my speech professor had probably ever experienced. In some ways, I felt sorry for her.

As a writer, as a storyteller, I am a human footnote, the earth passing up through my body until my throat is open and I am fully aware that even the air I breathe is not mine but everyone's. So I finally acknowledge my sources for that time so many years ago: thanks Dickie, Bob, Pat, Eugene, Chuckie, Frankie, Fred, Mike, and Kenny. I appreciate it. ℬ

Glossary

Age and character: At the heart of storytelling is an attempt to identify human qualities that eventually relate to the concepts of "age" and "character," qualities easily dismissed or disguised in a consumer culture burdened with convenience and superficiality.

Ambiguity: Generally refers to the fact that a situation is expressed in such a way as to recognize more than one possible interpretation. Like its counterpart, *irony*, it gives an experience more depth and authority, and sustains a more thoughtful analysis.

Background: The background of stories not only allows a reader context, but more often than not a means to experience the story itself, not separate from an incident, but an integral part of it.

Celebrity revelations: validating experience through celebrities—a trend that invalidates the stories of ordinary people because they do not seem "noteworthy" without the pomp that substitutes for legitimacy in a consumer culture fraught with endorsement via fame.

Commodity-driven identities: Designer t-shirts, the cars we drive, etc.—anything that speaks for us, or attempts to, in an inarticulate society hungry for self-expression.

Deviant moment: A "moment" that stands out, that makes one question and/or explore a routine. It is often the moment that inspires the story to be told, that alerts the storyteller to his or her source and the reader to the distinction that makes a story unique.

Fear of exclusion: The basis of alienation, the pressing fear that our experiences are not shared by others, which results in the antithesis of universality and empathy.

The feeling of oneness: Spanish writer Mario Vargas Llosa's term which describes the ability of storytellers to maintain a narrative stream of connectivity.

The grace of hesitancy: The author's term (originally written in a poem) to describe the trait that describes a moment of reflection and thought.

Grasp: To "grasp" a story as it unfolds (as it is told or written) the author implores the teller/writer, ironically, to let go, or to open up your memory and your imagination to allow details to nurture the often subconscious process.

Hero-worshipping without empathy: A process resulting from a popular culture tendency to assess character without depth or dramatic relevance.

Irony: Denotes a discrepancy between the intended meaning of an event or situation and the real meaning. Along with the word *ambiguity*, two terms essential to understanding the possibilities of human experience, the two terms are crucial to the vocabulary of young students.

Literary media analysis: A term to describe the interpretive analysis of popular media, such as commercials, TV. sitcoms, films, etc. Taking literary approaches to such media subjects and employing the kind of terms we have ascribed to literature in order to understand the creator's purpose and intentions.

Media display: The onslaught of media messages—visual, audio, and psychological—that overwhelms us on a daily basis.

Paradox: A term that fits into the same category as the words *irony* and *ambiguity* in this glossary, its exposure crucial to the understanding of storytelling and literature, especially for young students. Its meaning: a statement that seems contrary to common sense, and yet is perhaps true.

Physical context: A term that describes the textural details essential to create a sense of place and time, the background required in order for the story to emerge.

Primal narrative: The storyteller establishing a voice that utilizes qualities that are natural and universal to fundamental human expression.

Pseudo-narrative: A non-story that substitutes elements such as sensationalism and cliches for a probing and reflective narrative voice.

Selective detailing: Choosing details that are representational of the story's focus.

Sensual knowledge: The wisdom we acquire through human touch and direct encounters.

Storytelling Network Groups: Groups made up of ordinary people who meet to tell and write (sometimes employing local writers) their stories and sharing them with their local communities as well as communities throughout the country, connected through a central vehicle based on newsletters, internet communications, and other types of contacts.

Story-substitute: Something that looks like a story, feels like a story, sounds like a story (MTV videos, sit-com, special effects film, etc.), but which leaves us, although momentarily entertained, feeling left out and alienated, not connected to either the world around us or ourselves in any real or meaningful way.

Summaries and overviews: Generalizing to the point where we leave out or fail to rely on details that make a story vivid, immediate, and ultimately meaningful.

T. V. video narratives: A method of combining narratives from oral histories of ordinary people with a collage of photos and studio-produced background music to produce videos that can be seen on local T.V. news shows and other places.

Writers Block: Fear of words, of reflection, of conflict and complexity, fear of an honest appraisal of one's perspective on life.

Writer-in-Residence: A writer who adopts a social role in a community and helps others express themselves to enrich the community. To be effective, a true writer-in-residence must be just that, someone who lives among others, not the romanticized eccentric and isolated writer, but someone who serves others, perhaps best utilized by a city-government and sponsorships that are broad and diverse.

Immortal: For some reason I left this word out of this book. I don't have to explain what it means, and if you've read this far you know too it's the word at the heart of this book!

ROSS TALARICO

Award-winning writer and poet Ross Talarico has been at the forefront of enriching communities through writing, storytelling, and the utilization of writers in communal matters. His impact on others through his activist-approach to literature and his assessment of popular culture has led to keynote speeches at educational and literary conferences throughout the country, along with a nomination for a Presidential Appointment, and recognition as a writer who has rejected the idea that reading, writing, and sharing literature are isolated and elitist activities in our culture. This book, a sequel to his book Spreading The Word: Poetry and the Survival of Community in America, which was awarded the outstanding book of the year on literature and writing (The Mina P. Shaughnessy Prize, The Modern Language Association of America), brings together both Talarico's explicit advice on how ordinary people can create storytelling and literature that make a difference, and his eye-opening assessment of storytelling-substitutes that dominate our culture and divert our attempts to share our true identities. This book is filled with stories that remind us of who we are and where we came from and what's important to us. It also provides Ross Talarico's vision of a storytelling network of groups across the country sharing stories and strengthening both local and global communities.

Ross Talarico's writings have appeared in many publications, among them *The Atlantic, The North American Review, Poetry, Arts and Letters, New Letters, Prairie Schooner, The Nation,* and the *Iowa Review.* He is a professor of writing and literature at Springfield College, the San Diego campus. To contact Ross Talarico or inquire about storytelling network groups across the country, visit www.storytellingnetwork.com.